YIP
SANG

and the First Chinese Canadians

FRANCES HERN

HERITAGE

VICTORIA · VANCOUVER · CALGARY

Heritage House Publishing Company Ltd.
www.heritagehouse.ca

Library and Archives Canada Cataloguing in Publication
Hern, Frances
Yip Sang: and the first Chinese Canadians / Frances Hern.

(Amazing stories)
Includes bibliographical references and index.
Issued also in an electronic format.
ISBN 978-1-926936-90-1

1. Sang, Yip, 1845–1927. 2. Chinese—British Columbia—Biography. 3. Chinese—British Columbia—History. 4. British Columbia—Biography. 5. British Columbia—History—19th century. I. Title. II. Series: Amazing stories (Victoria, B.C.)

FC3850.C5H47 2011   971.1'004951   C2011-905029-3

Series editor: Lesley Reynolds.
Proofreader: Liesbeth Leatherbarrow.
Cover design: Chyla Cardinal. Interior design: Frances Hunter.
Cover photo: Like other prosperous Chinatown residents, Yip Sang wore both western and traditional clothing, depending upon the occasion. This photograph was taken in 1890. UBC Library, Rare Books and Special Collections, Wadd Brothers CC-PH-00254.

 The interior of this book was printed on 100% post-consumer recycled paper, processed chlorine free and printed with vegetable-based inks.

Heritage House acknowledges the financial support for its publishing program from the Government of Canada through the Canada Book Fund (CBF), Canada Council for the Arts and the province of British Columbia through the British Columbia Arts Council and the Book Publishing Tax Credit.

 Canadian Patrimoine
Heritage canadien
 Canada Council Conseil des Arts
for the Arts du Canada
 BRITISH COLUMBIA
ARTS COUNCIL

14 13 12 11   1 2 3 4 5
Printed in Canada

*For Karin, who said someone
should write a book about her great-grandfather*

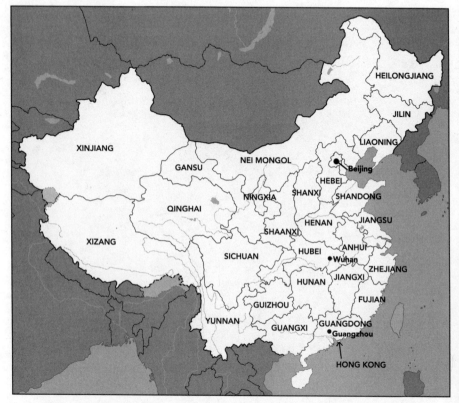

This map shows the mainland provinces and autonomous regions of China, including Guangdong Province, where Yip Sang spent his early years.

Contents

PROLOGUE 7

CHAPTER 1   The Gold Rush 9

CHAPTER 2   Building the Canadian Pacific Railway 16

CHAPTER 3   After the Railway 33

CHAPTER 4   A Family Man 48

CHAPTER 5   Mounting Discrimination 57

CHAPTER 6   Expansion and Restrictions 75

CHAPTER 7   The First Canadian-Born Generation 87

CHAPTER 8   The Second Canadian-Born Generation . . . 104

CHAPTER 9   Transition 121

EPILOGUE 130

SIGNIFICANT DATES IN CHINESE-CANADIAN HISTORY 135

CHINESE-CANADIAN PIONEERS 138

BIBLIOGRAPHY 140

INDEX 141

ACKNOWLEDGEMENTS 143

Prologue

STANDING ON THE DECK OF THE ship, 19-year-old Yip Sang *watched the hills of San Francisco draw closer. It had been 80 days since he'd left his home in Guangdong, a province on the southeast coast of China. He'd made his way to Hong Kong, where he'd boarded the Chinese junk that brought him to California. He smiled to himself as he recalled the gale that had blown up as they left Hong Kong. They'd been battling the winds for almost a week when he caught sight of city lights. Thinking that the gale had blown them to San Francisco in record time, he climbed to the upper deck for a first glimpse of California. To his great astonishment, he found that he was back in Hong Kong harbour. When the gale abated, they had set off again. Now, finally, he had reached Gum Shan—Gold Mountain. His new life was about to begin.*

It was an unusually clear day with no sign of the thick fog that often settled in the harbour. The remains of an old fort lay crumbling on top of one of the hills, and the young man could just make out the snowy peaks of the Sierra Nevadas in the distance. Vessels of all shapes and sizes were anchored in the bay ahead.

Yip Sang had been born on September 6, 1845, in the village of Shentang, Duhu County, in Guangdong Province. His father, Yip Yoon Yan, had died when Yip Sang was only a few years old. Now his mother was dead too, and his older sister was lost. She'd been abducted by local bandits, and he was resigned to the fact that he would never see her again. His family had scraped a living by weaving cotton fabrics, but locally made cloth now had to compete with low-priced western machine-made textiles. Yip Sang wanted more than a hand-to-mouth existence, so he'd sold almost everything he had to raise the money for his journey.

Yip Sang reached for the small bundle that contained all he owned in the world. Now his months of preparation and travel were at an end. His heart thumped in his chest as the sailors prepared the ship for their arrival. It was 1864, an exciting time to be in California, where men made fortunes prospecting for gold. Opportunities existed that he would never find back home in China. He had his whole life ahead of him, and he was going to make his fortune.

1

The Gold Rush

AS YIP SANG STOOD ON the dock in San Francisco, he found himself swaying as though he were still on the ship that had brought him across the North Pacific Ocean. He looked about. Most of the people had pale skin, although some were burned red by the sun. Some of them had unusually pale eyes, too, and hair that ranged in colour from the familiar black and grey through orange to straw. He tried to ask directions. The men growled replies he couldn't understand and waved him away with impatient gestures. Then he caught sight of a man with more familiar features. To his relief, the man spoke Cantonese. He pointed the way toward Chinatown, warning Yip Sang to watch out for the Yellow Line's horse-drawn trolleys and the inevitable mounds of horse dung that piled up in the streets.

Yip Sang wasn't the only person hoping to make his fortune in California. Sixteen years earlier, in 1848, James Marshall had discovered gold while building a sawmill near Coloma, 60 kilometres northeast of Sacramento. The owner of the land, John Sutter, tried to keep the find secret, but word soon got out, and local residents headed for the goldfields. Caught up in gold fever, office workers abandoned their desks and sailors deserted ships, leaving them anchored in the harbour with no one to sail them. As news of the gold discovery spread, travellers poured into California from Latin America, Europe, Australia, China and the rest of the United States. The population of San Francisco, which had numbered barely a thousand people, quickly swelled as forty-niners, named after the year of their arrival, erected tents and makeshift shelters.

With slavery abolished following the Civil War, earlier Chinese migrants to the United States had provided a welcome pool of cheap labour. They were recruited to build railroads, work mines and tend fields. By the time Yip Sang arrived in San Francisco, however, California's gold veins were drying up. American residents resented the continual arrival of foreigners wanting to find their gold and take their jobs. They particularly resented the Chinese, who were easily identified by their distinctive dress and features and had a reputation for working long hours for low pay.

At the beginning of the gold rush, California was still technically part of Mexico. Residents lived with an ever-changing mixture of Mexican rules and American principles, often interpreted to suit whomever was in charge at the time. Although California joined the Union in 1850, it took time to develop laws and ways to enforce them. It was not uncommon for disputes to be resolved personally and violently.

Given the increasing number of deaths caused by disease, accidents, malnutrition and growing ethnic tension, Yip Sang's story might have ended differently and much sooner had someone not taken the teenager under his wing. A man called Mr. Ing taught Yip Sang how to take care of himself in this new world. Yip Sang was so grateful that in later years, when his personal and financial situation had changed for the better, he tried to find Mr. Ing to thank him. He was unable to locate him but helped anyone named Ing who crossed his path, hoping to repay his debt of gratitude.

Under Mr. Ing's guidance, Yip Sang found work washing dishes and then cooking in a restaurant. He learned how to roll cigars, and he tried his luck in the goldfields. By now it was rare for individual prospectors to make money. It was the men who formed companies and were able to raise enough capital to buy expensive, heavy-duty equipment who made a profit. However, gold had also been found farther north, and many prospectors were moving on.

In 1856, a Nlaka'pamux (Thompson River Salish) man

had found a glittering pebble in the Thompson River, just a few miles upstream from the Thompson's confluence with the Fraser River at present-day Lytton. At the time, the site was known as The Forks. When the Native man found out how much Europeans treasured the shiny metal, members of his tribe began to collect it and trade it at Fort Kamloops. Other prospectors heard about the gold and arrived to search for it. James Douglas, who was in charge of the Hudson's Bay Company (HBC) in the district and also governor of Vancouver Island, was afraid that American miners would start to fight with the First Nations people and want to take over the land. He took charge of the settlement on the mainland and imposed British rule. Queen Victoria was called upon to name this territory. As Columbus had discovered the New World, and part of the area was already named Columbia on HBC maps, the queen decided to add the word "British." There would be no uncertainty about the ownership of this territory.

In 1858, 1,000 ounces of Fraser Canyon gold were sent to be processed at the San Francisco mint. When news of the gold's place of origin leaked out, the rush to the Fraser and Thompson rivers was on. The colony of Vancouver Island, which in 1854 was made up of approximately 450 settlers, rapidly ballooned with the arrival of thousands of miners, adventurers and prospectors wanting to try their luck along the Fraser, Thompson and Columbia rivers. This included the first influx of Chinese people to Canada, some of whom migrated from the California gold rush and some of whom came directly from China.

By the end of 1858, prospectors had staked out every single sandbar on the Fraser River, advancing upriver and along its many tributaries. The Fraser River gold rush was mostly over by 1860, but it was only the first of a sequence of gold rushes in British Columbia's interior and north. In 1862, an Englishman named Billy Barker found gold at the bottom of a deep shaft in Williams Creek in the Cariboo and hauled it out by the bucketful. One prospector in the 1885 Granite Creek gold rush, in the Tulameen River Valley, gathered up to $400 worth of gold a day. The last great gold rush occurred in the Klondike in 1896.

The gold being panned was placer gold, ground out of rocks by glaciers and weathering. It washed down the rivers and, being much heavier than water, settled out in sand or gravel bars, stream beds or alluvial fans. Unlike the gold in California, it didn't require expensive machinery or large groups of people to recover it. Anyone could find it, although the process required patience. Gravel was scooped up from the riverbed in a pan, which was then rotated in shallow water while held at an angle so that the gravel washed out, leaving sand and fine particles or flakes of gold, or if the prospector was really lucky, nuggets in the bottom of the pan. A rocker could also be used. This consisted of a short box on top of a longer one with coarse wire mesh between them. Gravel in the top box was rocked and washed with water so that finer particles passed through the coarse mesh to land on a piece of cloth above finer mesh that allowed water to drain away. The gold was removed from the cloth by brushing or washing, or sometimes the cloth was burned in a campfire and the gold picked out when the ashes had cooled.

Yip Sang Heads North

In 1881, at the age of 36, Yip Sang loaded his belongings onto a cart, joined a wagon train and trudged north through Oregon and Washington. He had succumbed to gold fever and decided to try his luck in the British Columbia goldfields. By this time, trails to the goldfields had been established; nevertheless, the journey was a hard one. Potential prospectors often underestimated what supplies they would need for their journey and starved or froze before they reached their destination. Of those men who did arrive, thousands were unable to stake claims. It was difficult to pan for gold when the rivers ran high, and impossible when they froze in winter. When they could work, prospectors were bent over with their hands in icy water for hours on end. The luckier ones lived in small wooden shacks with newspapers glued to the inside walls for insulation. A wood fire doubled as their cookstove. If they needed supplies, which were expensive, they might face a walk of many miles to reach the nearest town. If they wanted to eat, they had to soak and cook dried beans and bake their own bread. There was no medical help when men had accidents or were taken ill.

Chinese prospectors tended to follow their white counterparts. In these lawless places, it was every man for himself. Even men of the same nationality sometimes lied to, cheated and stole from each other, and the Chinese were well aware that they were not particularly welcome. Many of the white prospectors wanted to get rich quickly, so moved on if there was no sign of doing so. The Chinese then moved in to see what they could pan, content to make a good day's wage. Even so, they guarded their claims to stop others from jumping them, and they concealed any success to prevent robbery.

Yip Sang didn't find gold, but perhaps that was fortunate. If he had, he might have been cheated, robbed or even murdered. Instead, he eventually made his way to Vancouver, where he fed himself by selling sacks of coal from door to door. The coal-filled sacks were heavy, and by the end of each day he was covered in black coal dust. But at least he had somewhere dry to sleep, and he didn't have to walk miles to buy the makings of a meal. The following year his luck began to improve.

2

Building the Canadian Pacific Railway

YIP SANG HAD BEEN IN North America for 18 years when he met Lee Piu, who worked for the Kwong On Wo Company, which supplied the Canadian Pacific Railway (CPR). By this time, Yip Sang had taught himself English, and at the age of 37, he was no doubt eager to find better-paying work that required less brawn and more brain. Lee Piu hired Yip Sang to work as a bookkeeper, keep a record of employee hours and pay the men in his work gangs. This involved visiting various railway camps. Yip Sang rode a black mare and kept a revolver handy to protect his money bag.

According to family lore, his favourite route included a stop in Yale for apple pie served by a young Native girl. One evening when he stopped at Yale, a dance was in progress. When

Yip Sang asked what the special occasion was, he was told they were going to announce an engagement. Afraid that his love of apple pie served by a pretty young woman had given the wrong impression, he made a hasty departure. It wasn't that he didn't want a wife—he did—but he wanted a Chinese wife with Chinese values, and he already had someone in mind.

Yip Sang worked hard, and with his eye for opportunities, eventually negotiated the job of Chinese superintendent. This involved managing the flow of Chinese railway workers, many of whom came from his home province, Guangdong.

From Colony to Province

By the 1850s, the fur trade was winding down. The gold rush had brought the first Chinese to British Columbia, mostly from California, but when the frenzy died down in the 1860s, most of this first wave of Chinese immigrants left the colony. British Columbia was still rich in other natural resources but was isolated from the rest of British North America by thousands of kilometres and ranges of rugged mountains. The colony's inhabitants felt cut off from the men who governed British North America, as well as from eastern Canadian markets, both of which were an arduous and lengthy journey away. Mail destined for eastern Canada was routed through San Francisco and had to have an American stamp. Although British Columbia's population was still small, the colony's rapid growth had put it into debt, and government-funded services were needed.

Some people thought that British Columbia should join the United States. It was an expensive colony far from eastern Canada that already carried out much of its trade with the United States. However, politicians were busy working on the British North America Act, and on July 1, 1867, the Dominion of Canada was born. John A. Macdonald became Canada's first prime minister.

Macdonald and his supporters wanted Canada to extend from sea to sea and to include the vast western prairies for farmland and the still-valuable fur-trading territory of Rupert's Land, which made up the Hudson Bay drainage basin. The HBC had governed Rupert's Land since 1670, but the company was now in decline and ready to sell this huge area. The Americans were keen to buy it, but the British government insisted that Rupert's Land should be sold to Canada. In 1869, the land that now covers all of Manitoba, most of Saskatchewan, southern Alberta, southern Nunavut and northern parts of Ontario and Quebec was sold to Canada for £300,000. In 1870, after Manitoba and the North-West Territories joined New Brunswick, Nova Scotia, Ontario and Quebec in Confederation, delegates from the colony of British Columbia travelled to Ottawa to negotiate. The Canadian government promised that if British Columbia joined Confederation, the government would assume the colony's debt, provide money for public works, allow them to send six Members of Parliament to Ottawa and build a railway across the prairies and mountains to the Pacific.

What's more, they would complete the railway in 10 years.

The delegates were pleased at having negotiated what they wanted, and British Columbia became a province of Canada in 1871. However, the federal government had no idea how much this railway would cost or what route it would take through the mountains. Opponents claimed the idea was insane recklessness, arguing that the railway would be a massive undertaking that would cost thousands and thousands of dollars. They also argued that most of the land between British Columbia and Ontario was barely inhabited, and the new province was too geographically distant from the rest of Canada for proper communication with the east. British Columbia would have little political influence and be subject to policy decisions made far away.

Macdonald insisted the CPR would result in a great and united Canada. He also insisted on an all-Canadian route, although it would have been cheaper to avoid the rugged Canadian Shield by passing south though Wisconsin and Minnesota. To woo contractors, the government offered incentives that included vast grants of land in western Canada.

The Pacific Scandal
In 1872, Sir John A. Macdonald and other members of the ruling Conservative Party were involved in a controversy that became known as the Pacific Scandal. They had solicited election campaign funds from promoters, including Sir Hugh Allan, who headed the syndicate that was later awarded the

charter for building the railway. When news of this became public, the Conservatives were forced to resign, and Alexander Mackenzie, a Scottish stonemason, building contractor and newspaper editor, was asked to lead a new Liberal government.

Railway construction limped along. Surveyors argued over routes while Mackenzie began to construct segments under the supervision of the Department of Public Works. Canada's population was still less than four million people, and public money was in short supply, so progress was slow. But in 1878, Macdonald was returned to power. Whereas the Mackenzie government had promoted free trade, Macdonald promised to place significant duties on imported manufactured items, thus helping Canadian companies to sell their goods in the domestic market. He also promised to inject more energy into building the railway so that it could be finished in a timely fashion. He confirmed that the western terminus of the railway would be at Port Moody. Now a small city in Metro Vancouver, this port had been named after Colonel R.C. Moody, who arrived in 1858 to help establish the gold-rush community.

In 1880, the Macdonald government signed a contract with a group of businessmen that included George Stephen and Duncan McIntyre, both from Montreal. The syndicate agreed to connect the sections of railway built under government ownership and complete the railway within 10 years. Their price was $25 million and a grant of over 10 million hectares of land. Other concessions included waived import duties on all materials, waived taxes on unsold land and a ban on construction of competing railway lines for 20 years. To pick up the pace of construction, they hired William Cornelius Van Horne, who had worked in various capacities for American railway companies for 25 years. Van Horne was appointed general manager of the CPR and rose through the ranks to become the company's president in 1888.

In 1882, the first spike of the CPR was hammered just west of Bonfield, Ontario, to connect the recently built Central Canada Railway along the Ottawa Valley to the new line being built from the east. The CPR route across Ontario traversed the dense forest, muskeg and granite outcrops of the Canadian Shield. Its construction was far more challenging than building the prairie sections. However, the most difficult and dangerous part of the entire project was building the line through British Columbia.

The proposed route crossed land controlled by the Blackfoot First Nations; however, Albert Lacombe, a missionary priest, was able to persuade Chief Crowfoot, the Siksika leader, to allow the railway to proceed. The next problem was the Kicking Horse Pass. The steep drop west of the summit resulted in a seven-kilometre stretch of track with a 4.5-percent gradient—more than four times the recommended maximum gradient. As a result, runaway trains were a serious problem in the pass until the Spiral Tunnels were built 25 years later.

Another obstacle was finding a route through the

Selkirk Mountains. A surveyor named Major Rogers found the pass that was named in his honour, but the heavy annual snowfall caused many avalanches, and kilometres of snowsheds had to be built to protect the line. In addition, bridges had to be built across fast-flowing, icy rivers and canyons. Retaining walls were sometimes needed, and tunnels had to be blasted out of rock. In some locations, it was hard to find cover during the blasting, and labourers clearing away debris were exposed to rockfalls from above. Adding to the danger, fires often burned along the CPR's right-of-way. Andrew Onderdonk, an American of Dutch origin, was hired to supervise building the section of line from Vancouver. Despite the challenges, his work parties slowly moved east, reaching Eagle Pass in the Monashee Mountains, 19 kilometres west of Revelstoke, in 1885.

Working on the Railway

Building the railway took a lot of manpower, something that was in chronic short supply. Many of the first Chinese immigrants had departed in the 1860s with the decline of the Fraser River gold rush. To solve the problem, Onderdonk subcontracted through Chinese labour suppliers to bring men in from China. Yip Sang was one such supplier; between 1882 and 1885, he provided Chinese men to work on the railway between Port Moody and the Shuswap. Some of the men had worked in the United States constructing the Union Pacific Railway, but those who came directly from China had no experience. They were organized into groups of 30 men and boys, each group having one experienced worker or "bookman" who took charge and told them what to do.

This solution to the labour shortage was not welcomed by North Americans. The Chinese had gained a reputation for working long hours at low rates of pay, which made them unpopular with others looking for work. What's more, the Chinese lived frugally and either took much of what they earned back to China with them or sent it to support their families. This earned them the title of "sojourners," or *hua qiao*, since many of them intended to return home when they had saved enough money to improve their life in China. Even if they wished to stay in Canada, many people felt that the Chinese were too different to assimilate into the local population and adopt the lifestyle of other settlers from Europe and Britain.

In 1882, a resolution was proposed to induce CPR contractors to import and employ white labour instead of Chinese, but Onderdonk had already recruited several thousand Chinese men to build the mountainous section of the railway. Other bills to prevent Chinese immigration and regulate the Chinese population of British Columbia by taxing them for a work licence were disallowed and declared to be unconstitutional. Prime Minister Macdonald told Members of Parliament that they must choose between a railway largely built by Chinese labourers or no railway at all.

Although the Chinese were necessary to help build the

railway, many thousands of workers were needed, and they weren't all Chinese. All labourers had to pay for their own food, which they were charged for even if they were ill and did not eat. They were only allowed to buy clothing from company stores that charged inflated prices. They also had to pay for transportation costs and medical care and were not paid for days they missed work because they were ill, waiting for supplies or moving camp. In winter months, the snow and cold temperatures often brought work to a standstill. Tools consisted of shovels, picks, axes, drills, wheelbarrows and wooden ramps. But that was where the similarities between non-Chinese and Chinese workers ended.

While some railway workers were paid as much as $2.50 a day, the rate for the Chinese was $1 a day. They had agreed to this when they signed on, before realizing how many deductions would be taken out of their paycheques for food, shelter, days not worked, clothing and more. There was no logical reason for their lower pay. The Chinese labourers demanded fewer facilities, followed orders and were generally clean-living. They were able to move camp quickly and efficiently when it was time to start another section of the railway. Despite their generally small stature and slight build, they were often given jobs that were the hardest physically, such as felling huge trees and hauling away blasted rock on shifts that lasted from 8 to 10 hours a day. They were pressured to work quickly because of the limited budget, and safety measures were non-existent.

Chinese men work on the CPR tracks just west of Rogers Pass, British Columbia, in 1889. GLENBOW ARCHIVES NA-3740-29

Although workers of all backgrounds were sometimes at risk of being drowned, killed by rockfalls and cave ins, caught in explosions or avalanches, trampled by runaway horses, flattened beneath falling trees or attacked by bears or other wild animals, there were more deaths among the Chinese than other labourers. They were fed mostly rice and dried fish, and without any vitamin C in their diet, many suffered from scurvy. At first it was feared that the men had brought some horrible disease with them from China; yet even when it became clear that it was scurvy, which wasn't contagious, nothing was done about it. Without vitamin C, their bodies' connective tissue began to break down. Limbs swelled and teeth fell out. Their bodies bled and rotted. Death was painful, but few of the Chinese workers could have afforded to pay for medical help, even if it had been available. They suffered from the cold too. Having come from a milder climate, many did not own warm coats, hats and gloves, and labourers struggled to work barehanded when temperatures fell below zero.

They were lonely, ill-fed, often tired, sick and discouraged that they weren't able to save any money, yet the majority of them still stuck it out. Why did they do so? And why did their kinsmen continue to follow them to North America to work in such awful conditions?

Many of the Chinese labourers already in Canada were still repaying the cost of their passage from China and didn't have the money to go home. Most spoke little or no English, which made it difficult for them to cope on their own. Their families in China probably weren't told what their fathers, husbands and sons were going through. It's likely that these early immigrants, or *lao huaqiao*, didn't want to worry their relatives or admit that they weren't making any money, which would have caused an embarrassing loss of face. As bad as railway work was, in North America they had some chance of improving their lot, whereas in China they had none. They had initially given the name Gold Mountain to the North Pacific regions of North America because of the California gold rush in the 1840s, but over time that name came to mean simply finding prosperity. Migrants left China for the same reasons they left Scotland, Ireland and European countries; they were tired of war and ineffective or corrupt governments, or they couldn't find work and their families were starving.

Why the Chinese Came to Canada

China had been ruled by the Qing Dynasty, made up of non-Chinese Manchu people, since 1644. In 1839, the first Opium War began a series of wars with foreign powers. China's methods and equipment were outdated, and her rulers were forced to give out trading concessions and territory. The once self-sufficient Chinese felt humiliated, and many viewed their rulers as weak and corrupt. Local officials charged surtaxes to line their own pockets, and disgruntled groups of citizens felt it was time for change. A well-educated Hakka from northern China, Hong Xiuquan, began a rebellion against the Qing Dynasty after repeatedly failing the Imperial examinations that would have allowed him to enter government service and join the ruling elite. The Taiping Rebellion spread civil war throughout southern China from 1850 to 1864, and thousands died.

The central government did not have the resources to protect peasants from droughts, floods or bandits. The economy collapsed, which led to the spread of poverty and famine, especially in southeastern China. To make matters worse, China's population was growing rapidly. Between 1780 and 1850, Guangdong's population had doubled from 14 to 28 million. China had an agricultural economy with little industry. Peasant farmers divided their land into smaller plots with each generation. Even though south China's mild climate allowed them to grow two rice crops each year, farmers could not produce enough to feed everyone.

Many Chinese grew tired of their meagre existence, especially when they heard of the labour shortage in North America. Guangdong had a seafaring tradition, and its port of Guangzhou (Canton) had been a place of trade for foreigners for over 100 years. The men were used to venturing overseas to work in Southeast Asia and sending money home. Ironically, leaving China was considered un-Confucian. In 1712, the Chinese emperor had even declared that anyone returning after settling overseas should be beheaded. Sons were supposed to stay home, where they could honour their ancestors and continue the family line by having sons of their own. By the 1800s, however, working overseas had become a necessary fact of life. Many men left wives and children in China, whom they visited or returned to when they had saved enough money.

While one dollar a day in Canada was less than non-Chinese railway labourers were being paid, it was far more than the pennies, or *wén*, a man might earn in China.

Besides, many did not intend to leave China forever. If they worked hard for a few years and saved their money, they could return to China as self-made men. They had no idea how many unforeseen expenses would eat away at their hard-earned salaries, and so they continued to leave their families and make the long journey to Canada.

Yip Sang knew that the Chinese were badly treated, but he also knew how hard it was to earn a living in China. He had gambled on a new life, and it was paying off. If his countrymen were willing to risk working on the railway for a chance at a better life, then why wouldn't he, having journeyed to Canada in hopes of the very same thing, help them out? Of course, he was being paid to organize as many as 7,000 Chinese labourers who made up as much as 75 percent of the railway's workforce, and it's impossible to know if he had qualms about supplying workers or knew how dangerous the work could be. The bottom line was that the Chinese men wanted jobs, the Canadians needed men to build the railway and English-speaking Chinese were needed to organize the workers. If Yip Sang hadn't taken on the task, then someone else would have done so.

Macdonald's Dilemma

Despite the thousands of labourers toiling to complete the railway, blasting tunnels through mountains and building bridges across gorges and rivers was slow work. In 1884, the government passed the Railway Relief Bill and loaned another $22.5 million to the CPR. By 1885, the railway was almost complete, but Van Horne had once again run out of money. Macdonald faced a dilemma. Canada's debts were mounting and giving more money to the CPR would surely result in his Conservative party being voted out of office again. To allow the railway to flounder would leave it unfinished and trigger bankruptcies and corporate and personal hardships. Help came by way of a prairie rebellion.

The Metis, struggling to make the transition from hunting to farming, were upset that the new Dominion of Canada was not protecting their rights. They were joined by some disgruntled white settlers and Native groups who were also upset that the Canadian government was not giving them the help it had promised. In March 1885, the North-West Rebellion broke out in the district of Saskatchewan. Van Horne helped to transport Canadian troops west to quell the uprising. The miserable marches across snowy terrain in temperatures as low as -35°C took their toll, but by using the completed sections of railway, the troops reached Batoche on the South Saskatchewan River in record time. The Metis were overwhelmed, and their leader, Louis Riel, was captured. The general public viewed Van Horne and the CPR as the heroes of the day.

Many railway workers felt differently. The CPR had no money left to pay them. Groups of strikers tried to persuade other labourers who were still working to join them. Faced with riots and the impending bankruptcy of the CPR, Macdonald granted the railway company yet another loan.

The End of the Line

On November 7, 1885, with great ceremony, the last spike was hammered into the railway line at Craigellachie, 45 kilometres west of Revelstoke and east of the entrance to Eagle Pass. The massive project had been completed five years ahead of schedule. The CPR was soon operating at a profit and eventually paid off its government loans.

No one knows exactly how many men died while building the transcontinental railway. Some sources claim that as many as three or four Chinese died for every kilometre of track laid, but at the time, their deaths were thought to be of no consequence and were often omitted from accident reports. Families were not always notified when a death occurred, and agents did not necessarily pay the compensation that had been promised.

As sections of the railway were finished, labourers were laid off. The last of them were let go when the east and west sections were joined at Craigellachie, and the winter of 1885–86 took a particularly heavy toll on unemployed Chinese workers.

Most Canadians hoped the laid-off Chinese labourers would go home, and some did. Others stayed and searched for new jobs. Many had no choice because they didn't have enough money for the passage home, but with so many labourers being laid off during such a short time, finding work wasn't easy. Some settled in towns along the Fraser River. A few eventually moved east of the Rockies to settle in Alberta and beyond, finding work almost exclusively in laundries and restaurants. White employers would not hire them, and opening a laundry didn't require much capital. Besides, washing clothes and cooking were considered women's work, so the Chinese were not competing with other men for jobs. In British Columbia, however, they worked in mines and market gardens as well as in the lumber and fishing industries. Many flooded the Chinatowns of New Westminster and Victoria, but a Chinese district was also developing along the northwest shores of False Creek.

The CPR wanted the railway line to link up to its seagoing fleet and by 1885 had realized that the eastern end of Burrard Inlet at Port Moody was too shallow to accommodate ocean-going ships. In February 1885, a formal contract was drawn up that stated the railway line from Port Moody would be extended to Gastown in the immediate vicinity of Coal Harbour and English Bay. As soon as this decision became public knowledge, Gastown underwent a growth spurt. By 1888, the multicultural community had swelled to over 3,000 residents and over 1,000 buildings, including saloons, hotels and grocery stores that catered to mill workers, lumbermen, ships' crews and whalers. Officially renamed Vancouver, it was becoming Canada's most important west-coast port. The city was incorporated in 1886, and the first official train arrived there on May 23, 1887.

3

After the Railway

WITH THE RAILWAY COMPLETED, Yip Sang returned to China. His parents, Yip Yoon Yan and Lee Shee, had had three children, two sons and a daughter, and it's possible that Yip Sang visited his brother at this time. According to family lore, his brother had lent money to the government during the Taiping Rebellion. When the rebellion was over, he asked for his money back but was told that since he had lent it to a government official who had run away, the government had no obligation to pay it back.

Yip Sang's sister had been abducted by raiding Hakka tribesmen, who were involved in a clan war that began in 1855 with the Punti in Guangdong Province. Resentful of the fact that their growing population was forced to inhabit the hills and waterways, the Hakka tried to force other peoples off their fertile plains and helped the Imperial Army to raid Punti villages. The Punti retaliated by collecting Hakka heads. Captives were often sold to work as labourers in Cuba or South America, or to the brothels of Macau, a Portuguese colony bordering Guangdong Province to the south. Even if his sister was still alive, Yip Sang was unlikely to ever see her again.

Marriage

However, Yip Sang had another reason for returning to China. His family tell how, on an earlier visit, he had seen a young woman who had made such an impression on him that he had vowed to marry her. He was 40 years old now and could afford to support a wife and family. The young woman was still waiting, and they married. Lee Shee gave birth to a daughter, Gim Oy and a son, Kew Yue.

Unfortunately, Lee Shee became ill and unable to care for their children, so Yip Sang took a second wife. Lee Shee did not approve of his choice. This second wife, Wong Shee, was very young and inexperienced. Wanting to be sure that her children would be properly cared for, Lee Shee encouraged Yip Sang to find a third wife. Dong Shee, who was born in Macau, was more mature and capable of managing a household with children. Eventually, Yip Sang also took a fourth wife, Chin Shee, but there is no record of when or where they were married.

When a Chinese woman married, she was referred to by her maiden name. In the case of Yip Sang's wives, these were Lee, Wong, Dong and Chin. The term "Shee" was somewhat equivalent to "née" placed before a married woman's maiden name.

The Head Tax

It's unlikely that China's struggles to reform during the years Yip Sang spent in Canada had made life any easier for the common man. The elite members of the Qing Dynasty were resisting the change that the working people wanted. After three years, Yip Sang returned to Vancouver, leaving his wives and children in China. He was to visit China several more times during his lifetime and returned to Canada from his final voyage just before the outbreak of the First World War.

Even though the job situation in China had not changed enough by 1888 to entice Yip Sang to stay, life for the Chinese in Canada was not improving either. One of the first acts passed by the new Canadian province of British Columbia after it joined Confederation had been the Qualification and Registration of Voters Act of 1872, which stripped both First Nations people and the Chinese of the vote in provincial elections. Six years later, a law was passed in the province making it illegal for Chinese people to be employed on construction projects or other public works paid for by the provincial government.

While the CPR was being built, the Chinese provided essential labour. Now that it was finished, they were no longer wanted. In the same year that the railway was completed, the federal government passed the Chinese Immigration Act of 1885. As part of the British Empire, Canada was not allowed to shut down Chinese immigration entirely, but the government wanted to discourage it. According to the act, every Chinese person had to pay a duty before they were allowed to enter Canada. Anyone wilfully avoiding or attempting to evade this fee and anyone aiding or abetting such evasion was liable to a fine of up to $500, imprisonment for up to 12 months, or both. The act also set a limit on the number of Chinese immigrants each ship was allowed to carry. For each 50 tonnes of displacement, a ship could carry one Chinese immigrant. (As an example, Columbus's ship *Pinta* was approximately 50 tonnes in size.) The master of the vessel had to collect the duty payable before allowing any Chinese immigrants to leave his ship. Failure to do so resulted in a fine of between $500 and $1,000 for each offence, or imprisonment for up to 12 months and seizure of the vessel.

This duty became known as the head tax. When it was first introduced, the rate was $50 per person. Upon payment of the tax, the immigrant was given a certificate that included a head-and-shoulders photograph. Exceptions were made for members of the diplomatic corps or other government representatives and their staff, tourists, merchants, men of science and students carrying official documents verifying their identity, occupation and purpose for visiting Canada. This excluded most potential Chinese immigrants, who were only allowed into Canada upon payment of the tax.

Fifty dollars was a lot of money in 1885, and the majority of the Chinese had the lowest-paid jobs, if they found employment at all. Cannery workers were typically paid $25–$35 per month, while Europeans or British workers might be paid as much as $40 per month. Chinese labourers employed to build roads earned $15–$20 per month, while their non-Chinese counterparts earned $40 per month.

However, a head tax wasn't a new idea. Earlier in the 1800s, Nova Scotia had struggled to cope with the flow of Scottish immigrants arriving in Cape Breton. Many were destitute with little more than the clothes on their backs, and although some were supported by friends and relatives, others relied on government relief. The overwhelmed government was spending so much on immigrant aid that in 1832 it implemented a head tax of five shillings on any adult passenger or emigrant arriving in Canada from any port in the United Kingdom, with a reduced fee for children.

The Wing Sang Company

When Yip Sang returned to Vancouver in 1888, he set up business as a merchant and was thus exempt from paying the head tax. He called his import and export company the Wing Sang Company (Wing Sang means "everlasting" in

Cantonese). In 1889, Yip Sang built a two-storey building at 29 Dupont Street, now 51–69 East Pender Street, and the company's first export to China was 20 barrels of salted salmon.

Up until then, Chinatown's buildings had all been constructed from wood, but Yip Sang decided to build with bricks. Perhaps this decision was a reflection of one of the maxims by which he lived, which was to never do anything cheaply, presumably from a desire to acquire status. Or perhaps he wanted to keep his possessions and family safe; he no doubt had heard about the fire that had swept through most of the newly incorporated city of Vancouver three years earlier on June 13, 1886. It had begun with a brush fire, set alight to clear some land. A wind blew up, and the fire quickly spread out of control. It consumed all but a few buildings along False Creek and one or two others that were made of stone. Vancouver was quickly rebuilt, this time with a fire hall and water tanks. Even so, a brick structure was far less likely to go up in flames than a wooden one.

Yip Sang may have considered one more reason to build with brick. He was now 44 years old with children to provide for. If he had thought that a solid brick building would be an appropriate legacy to leave behind, he would be pleased to know that the Wing Sang Company building today has the distinction of being the oldest building in Vancouver's Chinatown.

Yip Sang holds the hand of his seventh son, Yip Kew Hong, outside the original Wing Sang Building, built in 1889. His sixth son, Yip Kew Gim, is second from the right. The Yip children wore traditional Chinese clothing until they started school. CITY OF VANCOUVER ARCHIVES 689-51, BAILEY BROS.

Situated in the heart of Chinatown but also conveniently close to the CPR terminal, the Wing Sang Company prospered. One odd feature of the Wing Sang building is the door on the second floor beneath the company name and date. Back in 1889, merchandise could be delivered by boat along False Creek at high tide. Goods were hoisted up and into the building through this door, which led into the conveniently located second-floor storeroom. Since then, this marshy area of False Creek has been drained and filled in, and today the building is some distance from the water. Another anomaly of the building is that the ground floor is slightly below the modern-day street level. In 1889, the sidewalks were made of boards placed above mud and gravel. When paved sidewalks were eventually installed, they were higher than the boardwalks, so that one now has to step down to enter the room off the street.

The main floor of the building contained a store and ticket office. Yip Sang became a Chinese passenger agent for the CPR, a lucrative position that he held for the rest of his life. He sold tickets for the steamship line and handled both passenger and freight traffic. He also imported Asian products through business agents in Hong Kong. Employees used an abacus to record accounts and prepare invoices. Although Yip Sang taught himself English, he wasn't very literate so employed an English and a Chinese secretary. When the English secretary read his letters back, they were in perfect, grammatically correct English with all traces of English and Chinese swear words removed.

Inside the store was a thick counter that measured three metres or more in length. In later years, the young boys in the family liked to sit there while waiting for a parent, a feat that became easier as they grew taller. The store's shelves had glass doors and rose all the way to the ceiling. These shelves were packed with brown-paper packages tied with string and marked with Chinese characters in black ink to identify the contents. The packages contained warm padded vests and jackets worn by contract work crews. Instead of buttons, the jackets had knobs made from knotted cord that fitted into loop fasteners. There were stacks of Chinese-style stand-up collars that could easily be sewn onto jackets by Chinatown tailors who worked on a piecework basis. There were bolts of silk, decorative trims, trinkets and curios, and pairs of shoes that were all the same but in different sizes. The Wing Sang Company also sold gas mantles, tooth powder, bamboo combs and provisions such as rice, ginger and condiments. Cooking utensils included rice mills and bamboo rice-winnowing screens that were used to separate grain from chaff.

The company also sold ceramic opium-pipe bowls, which were easily broken and needed to be replaced regularly. The bowl sat partway down a bamboo stem, through which the smoke was inhaled. Heated opium was placed in a small hole in the top of the pipe bowl and smoked. The company also imported and sold opium, which was not illegal when Yip Sang first established the Wing Sang Company.

In fact, by 1891 Chinatown had numerous opium dealers and factories. One factory, the Hip Tuck Lung Company, was located across the street from the Wing Sang Building. Until 1908, Chinese merchants could sell opium legally if they purchased the appropriate city licence for $500. There were reports that non-Chinese people used the opium dens too, and city officials sometimes raided Chinatown looking for unlicensed establishments that were selling the drug.

The Opium Wars

Opium had been used as a painkiller and to treat conditions such as diarrhea for hundreds of years, but it was highly addictive, and its effects could be devastating. Men who smoked opium spent hard-earned wages on the drug, often neglected their families and, if they smoked heavily, usually died within a few years. In 1729, after seeing more and more of his people wasted by the drug, the Chinese emperor Yongzheng banned the smoking of opium. He allowed only a small amount to be produced under licence for use in medicines, and this ban kept the opium situation in China under control for almost 100 years.

By the beginning of the 1800s, China's external trade was brisk. Porcelain, silks and particularly tea were exported in large quantities. The country was virtually self-sufficient. The Chinese had little interest in western products they considered to be shoddy and wanted to be paid for their tea and silks in silver. The British were running out of silver, and their trade deficit with China was rapidly rising. They needed something they could sell to the Chinese—something the Chinese wanted so badly that they would purchase it with silver rather than simply exchange goods. One commodity the British had in abundance was opium, which was grown in India by the British East India Company.

The British began to ship opium to southern China. To get around the import ban, British merchants bought tea in Canton on credit and, to balance their books, sold opium at auction in Calcutta. The buyers hid the opium aboard British ships and sailed to the Chinese coast, where they met up with Chinese merchants who smuggled the opium into China. Between 1816 and 1830, the quantity of opium shipped into China increased significantly each year.

Despite the previous emperor's ban, millions of Chinese were becoming addicted to the drug. This led to economic and social problems. The English would only accept payment in silver, which was now flowing out of instead of into China. Drug addicts resulted in lost productivity, and if men didn't work they couldn't pay taxes. With less income from taxes, the government was unable to carry out its normal functions. There was also a shortage of capital for investment and a rise in crime. Repeated protests to the British had no effect, and so Emperor Daoguang appointed radical patriot Lin Zexu to the position of Chinese Commissioner.

Lin Zexu was determined to stamp out the opium trade. He made hundreds of arrests in Guangzhou and confiscated thousands of pounds of opium from the ship- . ping warehouses. He dumped the opium into a large trench, added lime to make the burning more effective and less dangerous, and set it ablaze. He ordered troops to board British ships in international waters and destroy any opium on board, even when the ships were outside Chinese jurisdiction. He tried to turn back English merchant vessels. The British claimed that these actions violated their right to free trade, and the friction resulted in the First Opium War of 1839–42.

Chinese weapons were no match for British gunships and armies that were better equipped with more modern technology and methods. The Chinese suffered a humiliating defeat and, in 1842, were forced to sign the Treaty of Nanking. This treaty required China to open five treaty ports for trade. It fixed customs duties at a low rate that left the country's industries open to competition from cheap imports, such as machine-made fabrics from Britain that cut into the demand for hand-woven textiles, like those made by Yip Sang's mother and sister. Western merchants no longer had to operate through the *cohong*, a guild of government-authorized Chinese brokers. China was also forced to pay an indemnity and cede Hong Kong to Britain for 100 years. An additional treaty stated that British citizens in treaty ports were subject to British rather than Chinese law.

A second opium war occurred from 1856 to 1860. Once again, China was defeated and forced to open new treaty ports and pay indemnities to Britain and France. Kowloon, on the mainland, was surrendered to the British, and foreigners, including missionaries, were to be allowed to travel through China. These consequences of the opium wars meant that China lost the ability to regulate trade in her ports, and it was no longer illegal to import opium.

Opium was first brought into Canada in the many ships that unloaded silks from China and took on cargoes of timber. The Chinese who made their way to Vancouver in the late 1800s were all too familiar with the drug. Far from home and family and finding their activities restricted by discrimination, many Chinese men were lonely and had little to do when they weren't working. In 1860, Mrs. Kwong Lee, the wife of the owner of the Kwong Lee Company in Victoria, became the first Chinese woman to arrive in British North America, but few men could afford to bring their wives to Canada, especially with the new head tax. Unhappy and unable to return home, the men found that smoking opium or sniffing morphine were among the few pleasures in their lives. It helped them to escape the reality of their poorly paid and lonely lives for a little while. Opium was also an effective painkiller for those unwilling to buy unfamiliar western medicines.

Between 1886 and 1889, the opium habit slowly spread to the white population. By 1887, the chief constable reported that about 50 white opium users in Vancouver, who made up 1 percent of the population, were beyond redemption.

Salt Herring

Although Yip Sang and the other merchants of Chinese origin came from rural backgrounds, they were familiar with free-market capitalism, which flourished in China. They also spoke Cantonese and could help to establish lucrative business connections in Asia. The fact that they were recognized to be a valuable component of western Canada's economy was reflected in the fact that they were not required to pay the head tax for family members joining them in Canada.

Despite this, Chinese entrepreneurs had to make their money as middlemen. They faced many obstacles when they tried to set up businesses, as westerners did not want the Chinese competing with them and undercutting their prices. Many of them didn't want to do business with the Chinese either—they just didn't understand or trust them.

A Chinese merchant named Chang Toy ran an import and export business in Vancouver's Chinatown called the Sam Kee Company. Chang Toy and Yip Sang were always on the lookout for business opportunities and saw a niche in the salt herring business.

By the 1890s, Japanese migrants formed a significant proportion of the workforce that fished along Vancouver's coastline and worked on shore packaging and canning fish. At the time, there was very little commercial demand for herring, and so the Japanese owners and operators were able to start up a small business selling herring that had been soaked in brine and then dried. But it wasn't easy;

they often lacked the cash needed to buy salt and packing crates, and they didn't have the overseas contacts necessary to find buyers.

Both the Wing Sang and Sam Kee Companies were well established by this time. At first, they helped with shipping and handling. They were able to provide supplies on credit and help find markets for the herring. As demand for the preserved herring increased, Yip Sang also began to export salted chum and keta salmon. He formed the Nanaimo Packing Company Ltd. in 1909, where fish for export were packed into barrels with "Packed in Canada" stencilled on the sides.

While Chinese-Canadian businessmen were tolerated as middlemen, they had long since learned that it was better not to advertise their ownership of business ventures. This was reflected in the names they chose, such as the English-sounding Nanaimo Packing Company Ltd. The company owned two plants for dried salted herring, one in the town of Nanaimo and the other north of Nanaimo at Nanoose Bay. The Nanaimo plant burned down in 1910, so Yip Sang bought another in Departure Bay, on Newcastle Island, to replace it. He tore this plant down in 1911 and rebuilt it, and in 1913 he built another on Galiano Island. The plants were successful, and by 1923 he estimated they were worth $23,600.

A Family Man

IN 1891, YIP SANG BECAME a naturalized British subject. With his business up and running, he extended the Wing Sang building. The original storefront was just over six metres wide, but in 1901 he added three more street-level shops with second floors and added a third storey above both the original building and new extension. He also arranged for his wives and children to join him in Vancouver. His first wife, Lee Shee, had died in China, but Dong Shee, Wong Shee and his children moved into the new residence in 1901.

Polygamy

Although most ordinary Chinese citizens were monogamous, traditional Chinese culture neither prohibited nor advocated polygamy. Emperor Qianlong, who ruled China from 1735 to 1796, banned all non-patrilineal inheritance, which meant that only a son could inherit a man's possessions. To help prevent the wealth and property of a man without sons from passing to outsiders, the emperor also allowed polygamy. Naturally, having more than one wife increased the number of children a man was likely to father, as well as his chances of having sons and heirs who survived childhood. Sons were highly valued as they carried on the family line, and wives who were unlucky enough to bear only daughters were looked down upon by other members of the community. Daughters did not receive any inheritance when a grandfather or father died. The Chinese had a saying: Boy don't be born last (because there might be nothing left to inherit) and girl don't be born first (because she would have to do all the work).

Having more than one wife was also prestigious. It showed that a man had the means to support a larger family. Polygamy was eventually banned by the Republic of China's government in 1930, but Canada's first laws against polygamy were passed in 1890, so Yip Sang would not have been able to legally claim that Dong Shee and Chin Shee were wives. As a merchant, however, he may have been able to avoid paying the head tax, which in 1900 had been raised to $100, to bring them into Canada.

Wong Shee became Yip Sang's second wife after Lee Shee became ill and unable to care for their children. In this 1910 portrait, she wears formal Chinese attire, which was made from silk, satin, brocade and velvet. UBC LIBRARY, RARE BOOKS AND SPECIAL COLLECTIONS, KING STUDIO EX-8-3

Wong Shee and Dong Shee may have viewed the idea of leaving their home to move to Canada with a sense of adventure or one of alarm. There was a chance they would never see the rest of their families again, and given the situation in Canada, they were also likely to be treated with less respect in their new country. There was also the journey itself to consider. Would they have to walk far? And with bound feet, how would they manage to keep their balance aboard a swaying ship?

Foot Binding

The tradition of foot binding began among women at the imperial court and, surprisingly, included court dancers. It spread through the ranks of the wealthy as a status symbol indicating that the woman's husband had the means to provide for her and she did not have to work. Eventually, the custom even spread among poor women hoping to improve their status by marrying a man with money or a high position in society.

When a Chinese man wanted a wife, it was traditional for a matchmaker to find a suitable young woman. The matchmaker would arrange for a foot viewing, and the man would go to the young woman's house for the sole purpose of looking at her feet. If he thought they were too large, he would turn her down. This caused much embarrassment, especially as the entire village usually found out.

The process of binding began in girls, sometimes as young as four years old, before the arch of the foot was fully developed. The three smallest toes were broken and folded around the side of the foot so that they pressed tightly into the sole. The arch of the foot was also broken and bound so that the big and second toes curved towards the heel, forming a five-centimetre crevice where the arch of the unbound foot would have been. It took two years to reduce the foot to a length of approximately eight centimetres from toe to heel in the shape of a crescent moon, the so-called Golden Lotus. Unable to place their heels down and roll forward onto the toes, women with tiny, bound feet were forced to take small steps with a swaying "Lotus Gait" that men found alluring.

It could take years for the girls to learn to walk again. For some women, the pain eventually went away; others experienced pain and difficulty walking all their lives. Feet had to be bound day and night to maintain their shape and size. The communists of the new Republic of China finally outlawed foot binding in 1911. Many women who tried to go without the support of binding cloths found it excruciatingly painful and difficult to walk. Some were reduced to crawling on their hands and knees, and most resumed binding their feet.

Family Life
Yip Sang's family settled into their new home with Dong Shee assuming the position of number one wife, or First Lady. While it was common for the first wife in a polygamous relationship to have the most prestige, Yip Sang's first wife, Lee Shee, had died, and Dong Shee, who was chronologically

his third wife, was deemed most capable of running a busy household. Yip Sang tried to be fair and spend equal time with his three remaining wives, Dong Shee, Wong Shee (Second Lady) and Chin Shee (Third Lady). They began to produce half-brothers and half-sisters for Lee Shee's son and daughter.

Family was very important to the Chinese. Like the Scots, a clan linked families of one surname, or those of several surnames tied through history. Clan members who worked overseas were expected to contribute to the well-being of their clan by sending money home, and even when they weren't acquainted, immigrants with the same family name banded together and looked after each other. They took care to see that a kinsman was properly buried and helped each other find work. For example, if a Chinese Canadian from a different clan was employed in a family-run restaurant or store, they were likely to be fired if a member of the owner's family needed a job. Businessmen also raised capital by borrowing from their clan or pooling funds with other clan members.

Confucius, a Chinese philosopher born in 551 BCE, likened the family to a living tree. Family members represent branches and leaves. If each thrives, then the entire tree prospers. At the end of its life, the leaf or branch falls to the ground, decomposes and nourishes the tree's roots for another cycle of birth and death. If each branch and leaf does its part, the tree grows and thrives until it casts a soothing shade for the entire neighbourhood to enjoy.

With clan ties being so important, the traditional form of address in China began with the last or family name. The family name Yip means "green leaf." Yip family middle names were a generation name predetermined by ancestors. The generation name of Yip Sang's sons was Kew; his daughters' was Gim. His sons' sons had the generation name of Wing, and his sons' daughters were May. His daughters' children were named according to their husband's family. Traditionally, an individual's name was expressed last, but as the younger generations adapted to western customs they reversed the order and placed their surname last.

While the generation name made it easy to know who was an uncle or a cousin, the system was complicated by the fact that individuals were often given a new name upon reaching an important benchmark in their lives, such as graduating from school, going into business or getting married. Yip Sang was also known as Yip Chun Tien, Yip Lin Sang and Yip Loy Yiu. In Mandarin, his name translated as Ye Sheng. In addition, family names came first rather than last, which must have been confusing for Canadian authorities and no doubt sometimes worked to an individual's advantage.

The Chinese naming system also makes it difficult to trace records, especially in the case of married women known only by their maiden family name, as were Yip Sang's wives. It can be difficult to find the gravesites of ancestors too. Even if the Chinese character for the name is known, the old classical style of calligraphy was simplified by the People's

Republic of China during the 1950s and 60s, with useless strokes omitted. As a result, some characters are still recognizable, others are not. Also complicating the search for ancestors, some old Chinese villages have grown in size and merged with others, so it can be hard to locate the village in which a gravesite is located.

Expanding Business

As Yip Sang's family expanded, so did his business, and the Wing Sang building became a busy part of Vancouver's Chinatown. As well as selling everyday items, customers wanting to send remittances or money to China could deposit it in the Wing Sang Company branch of a trust company based in Hong Kong. Labourers could do so on a Sunday, their only day off. This was very convenient because western banks were closed on Sundays. It was also convenient for the merchant, who could use the money to buy export goods for sale in China and pay the remittances from part of his profit.

Yip Sang's customers could also collect mail from China. The Canadian postal system was not able to deliver letters addressed in Chinese characters, so these were dropped off at the Wing Sang building, where they were picked up by their intended recipients. Even men who worked in lumber or mining camps or fish canneries eventually passed through Vancouver, or someone who worked with them did, and although it sometimes took a long time, many of these letters eventually reached the addressees.

The Wing Sang Company sold tickets to passengers on CPR steamships and supplied the ships with both vegetables and sailors. The CPR had the foresight to purchase the Canadian Pacific Navigation Company and add more ships to this coastal fleet. The steamships sailed between Vancouver, Victoria and Seattle, and also up the British Columbia coast to the Alaska panhandle, making deliveries along the way to many isolated ports. Sir William Cornelius Van Horne, who had received a knighthood in 1894 for his accomplishments, had also purchased three luxury ocean liners from Cunard and in 1887 began a trans-Pacific service from Vancouver to Asia. By 1891, the liners *Empress of China, Empress of Japan* and *Empress of India* were carrying passengers, tea and silk from Asia. They also became Royal Mail ships and carried mail between Britain and Hong Kong via Canada.

When Yip Sang wasn't busy, he often sat beside the stove in the store wearing a hand-embroidered skullcap with a decorative button in the centre. From here he was able to keep an eye on his family's comings and goings and invite customers to drink tea or share a smoke of tobacco from a water pipe. He also could debate China's political future, the merits of the latest opera or give out information on how to enrol a child in Chinese school. Despite his lack of formal education, Yip Sang was becoming a highly successful and well-known member of the community. However, many Chinese immigrants found life in Canada more difficult.

5

Mounting Discrimination

BY THE END OF THE 19th century, Chinese immigrants in Canada made up a much-needed migratory, all-male, seasonal work force. Because they did not demand higher wages, Chinese workers made it possible for Canada to produce commodities at a competitive price. However, this undercutting of non-Chinese workers led to resentment from the other nationalities that were part of the multicultural Canadian population.

The Chinese were looked down upon because they were often forced to live in low-rent, dilapidated and crowded buildings and formed large bachelor communities because they couldn't afford to—or weren't allowed to—bring their families to Canada. It didn't help that a group of non-Chinese prostitutes moved to Shanghai and Canton alleys when they were evicted from another part of the city. The Chinese Board of Trade, formed to protect Chinese businessmen, protested, and the prostitutes eventually moved on. However, mixed marriages between Chinese and non-Chinese, or *lo faun*, were met with great disapproval. There were very few single and eligible women of Chinese origin in Vancouver. The ratio of Chinese men to women in 1911 was 28:1; by 1931, it was still only 12:1. Without any opportunity to marry, or with wives left in China, men did sometimes pay for a prostitute's services.

Because of the way most were forced to live, the Chinese were not perceived as hardworking people who wanted a better life than the one they had left behind in China. They were viewed as foreigners from a poor and backward country who had low moral standards that included gambling and smoking opium. They were uneducated, didn't speak English and crammed as many men as they could into run-down buildings without proper bathroom facilities, where germs might multiply. They lived frugally and sent their wages back to their families in China. They congregated in groups and chattered excitedly in a strange language.

Canadians of British or European origin wanted settlers who would blend into the population, immigrants who looked like themselves, lived like themselves, spoke English and had similar customs, traditions and values. Racism against the Chinese was mounting, but provincial and federal governments refused to help. Government officials were looking for settlers for the prairies, and they preferred stalwart peasants in sheepskin coats, whose forefathers had been farmers for 10 generations and who had stout wives and half a dozen children. Chinese immigrants realized that they would have to work together to try to diffuse anti-Asian sentiment.

The Chinese Benevolent Association

In the summer of 1884, a group of Chinese merchants in Victoria had formed the Chinese Consolidated Benevolent Association, partly in response to anti-Chinese racism and partly to help their fellow countrymen. The association fought discriminatory laws and helped destitute workers who wanted to return to China. In 1891, the association collected the remains of several hundred Chinese railway workers from graves in the Thompson and Fraser canyons and shipped them home to China for burial.

The practice of secondary burial was traditional in southern China. The deceased were buried for several years to allow soft tissues to decompose. Amidst burning incense or lit candles, the remains were then dug up in the presence of a son or other male relative. Paper money was also burned, or sometimes firecrackers were lit to celebrate this transformation of the deceased. The relative knelt to receive the bones, which were cleaned with rice wine before being wrapped with one limb, the ribs or a set of phalanges in separate gauze bundles or packets. Vertebrae were threaded together to reconstruct the spinal cord. The bones were then carefully arranged in a fetal position inside a final sealed tomb or jar. The ceramic jars, approximately 45 centimetres high and 30 centimetres wide, were kept in a special building in the village.

The Chinese who came as sojourners and died in Canada wanted their remains returned to their homeland, where they could rest amongst their ancestors. Even those who settled in Canada permanently often requested that they be sent home when they died. Accustomed to secondary burial rites, the Chinese had no qualms about digging up corpses, even from cemeteries, as this provided a relatively simple and inexpensive way to comply with a person's last wishes to be sent home. In fact, they often labelled corpses before they were buried, or took the time to mark gravesites, so they could later identify the deceased and know which village to send them to. Westerners found this desecration of graves distasteful, and it gave them one more reason to dislike the Chinese.

A few years after Victoria's benevolent association was formed, Yip Sang helped to found a similar Chinese Benevolent Association in Vancouver. The association looked after ill, elderly or destitute Chinese who had no family in Canada. It provided shelter, a place to meet and emergency help, and also acted as an unofficial employment agency. It marked ancestral days and festivals, and members knew that if they died in Canada, their funerals would be properly arranged.

The association also helped to settle disputes within the community. This was important because the Chinese traditionally avoided contact with police whenever possible, and some even believed that visiting a police station would bring bad luck. Perhaps this was because contact with Chinese authorities was often a negative experience, or because they felt they wouldn't be treated fairly in Canada. Or it may simply have been that in China they were used to appealing to the elders or heads of the village to resolve conflicts. Elected elders were trusted to be fair and had the wisdom that age could confer. Just as the people would have accepted the decisions of village elders, they accepted the decisions of the benevolent association's committee.

In the longer term, the association also worked to promote equality for Chinese Canadians and foster better understanding with groups of different ethnic origins.

The Chinese Freemasons Society

During these early years, the Chinese Freemasons Society (known as Chee Kung Tong in Cantonese) also set out to help new immigrants from China. The Chinese Freemasons were not affiliated with western freemasonry; however, they too had a somewhat secretive background. Although members were supposedly dedicated to overthrowing the Manchu Qing Dynasty, some groups, or *tongs*, began to operate gambling parlours, opium dens and brothels using girls brought from China, all of which became illegal in

North America. Gangs fought to control territory, and disagreements between the Freemasons and Dr. Sun Yat-sen's Chinese Nationalist League later resulted in tong wars in various Canadian cities, so many Chinese Canadians tried to avoid the society.

Evangelical Christians also worked to steer immigrants away from liquor, opium, gambling and prostitution, offering them sympathy and help through English classes. Some Chinese converted to Christianity, despite the lack of love and brotherhood demonstrated by many so-called Christians.

Continuing Unrest in China

The Canadian government responded to increasing friction between oriental and occidental citizens by trying to slow the flow of Chinese and Japanese immigrants into Canada. In 1903, the head tax payable by immigrants from both countries was raised to $500 per person. It could take one family 14 years to save this much money, which was enough to buy two houses. Immigrants arriving in Victoria from Hong Kong were moved to a building nicknamed the "Pig House" while they were processed. If a large number of immigrants arrived at the same time, this processing could take up to one month, although a bribe could speed up the proceedings. Even so, those who could afford to pay the head tax were willing to take their chances in Canada. The situation in China was dire.

Mounting Discrimination

The Opium Wars had shown that western powers were stronger and better equipped than China. During the 1870s and 1880s, China had undergone the Self-Strengthening Movement—an attempt by the Qing rulers to modernize their military, improve relations with western powers and learn about western advances in science and technology. Despite these efforts, China lost control of Korea in the First Sino-Japanese War (August 1894–April 1895). With this defeat had come the realization that while Japan had successfully modernized, China had not. China was no longer the centre of the world, or even the centre of East Asia. Japan now dominated the area. This was one humiliation on top of another, and the ordinary Chinese people demanded reform.

Emperor Guangxu agreed that they had to do something to reverse the deteriorating state of the country. He began to issue edicts that would modernize schooling, food production and transportation. He wanted to eliminate bribery and corruption. However, the Chinese elite were less willing to give up old ways. The Dowager Empress Cixi took charge and ordered Guangxu put under house arrest. Several of his top reformers were executed, while others fled.

Meanwhile, another peasant movement, which became known as the Boxer Rebellion, had been gaining strength in rural China. Its members wanted to free China from the control of barbarian foreigners. Influenced by Christian missionaries, they believed that training in spiritual and physical exercises would allow them to prevail. Because these young men trained with martial arts and calisthenics, they were called Boxers. They had originally intended to overthrow the imperial government, but after some hesitation, the Dowager Empress Cixi encouraged them and gave them support. In 1900, the Boxers besieged the foreign embassies in Beijing. In response, eight nations (Austria-Hungary, France, Germany, Japan, Russia, Italy, the United Kingdom and the United States) sent an allied force to rescue their nationals. This army occupied Beijing on August 14, 1900. The dowager empress, emperor and other officials fled. The eventual settlement resulted in an expanded open-door policy in China that allowed foreign access until the Second World War.

Vancouver's Growing Chinatown

Between 1901 and 1911, Vancouver's population quadrupled from 30,000 to 120,000 inhabitants. Chinatown was expanding too, and like San Francisco's Chinatown a few decades earlier, had become a social and economic centre for Chinese traders, consumers, workers and investors, as well as a cultural refuge. In 1910, Vancouver's Thomson Stationery Company published a phrase book for Chinese newcomers. It included standard English phrases that would be useful when paying the head tax, finding work in laundries, mines or sawmills, and during emergencies, such as being placed under arrest. Most of Chinatown's buildings were constructed between 1910 and 1920, and it was virtually self-contained. The inhabitants formed numerous associations for help and support, and buildings included schools, a hospital, a library and a theatre.

In 1898, the 500-seat Sing Kew Theatre was built near the bustling Shanghai Alley. The alley was first listed in Vancouver's city directory as Shanghai Street in 1906. The theatre was used for political and cultural activities, including meetings, debates, plays and the very popular Chinese operas.

Along with other Chinatown merchants, Yip Sang became a patron of the arts. He collected librettos and sponsored performances of travelling Chinese-opera troupes. Performances often lasted as long as four hours, but everyone knew the stories, and audience members could come and go as their schedules and tolerance for opera permitted. The colour of an actor's makeup or face paint depended upon the role he was playing. Heroes wore red or black makeup, gods wore gold or silver and comic characters wore white or yellow. Children were usually admitted free of charge, while adult prices ranged from 25 cents to $1.50, depending upon how much of the performance they had missed. Although this was entertainment for the whole family, men sat separately from women and children, and children could move around and visit with friends when they grew tired of sitting. Sometimes a portion of the entrance fee was donated to support an organization or cause in China.

Yip Sang formed a syndicate of merchants to develop a Chinese-style courtyard adjacent to the Sing Kew Theatre. Constructed in 1904, the courtyard, a narrow passageway, had a row of buildings along either side, and the only entrance was fitted with an iron gate for security. This became known as Canton Alley. The buildings had shops on the main floor with apartments, boarding houses and meeting halls above them. The residences were filled with men who could not afford to pay for their families to join them in Canada, and every inch of space was put to use in the tiny apartments. Firewood was stored beneath the beds, and fish were tied up to dry on the fire-escape railings. There were no bathrooms, but for a small fee the occupants could use the facilities in the nearby Sam Kee Company building. The apartments were rarely empty. Seasonal workers would rent their beds to other men while they were away, and workers on different shifts sometimes shared beds. Shanghai and Canton alleys were the bustling centre of Chinatown life until the mid-1920s. Shoppers visited the tailors, grocers, barbers and cobblers, while children played or searched for lumps of coal along the adjacent railway tracks. In the evenings, appetizing smells wafted from restaurants. Music from the theatre could often be heard a block away, along with clanging bells from passing trains and excited outbursts from groups playing mah-jong, blackjack or fantan.

By the beginning of the 1900s, there were about 15,000 Chinese residents in British Columbia. Many were employed in lumber mills, in fish canneries and on steamships, while others worked as servants for wealthy families, with as many as 260 Chinese houseboys employed in the city, many in Shaughnessy mansions. Servants earned between $10 and $30 a month and lived in rooms in the basement. They worked long hours and were summoned by call boxes that indicated which of the approximately 20 rooms in the house they were to hurry to. The Chinese also worked as tailors, porters and clerks, and in laundries and restaurants, although it was not uncommon to see signs such as "Snappy Service–Home Cooking–All White Help." They grew and delivered vegetables, but were fined if they were found selling them door-to-door. Storekeepers had complained that this practice forced them out of business, and in 1894 a law had been passed that allowed only permanent places of business to sell fresh food. However, this law was difficult to enforce.

Employers of Chinese labourers found that, for the most part, they worked hard, were reliable and tended to remain with the same employer. However, they still encountered discrimination. The majority of entrepreneurs interviewed during a royal commission in 1901 felt that since British Columbia was now connected to the rest of the country by rail and there were more white labourers, the Chinese were no longer useful.

A Chinatown Riot
In the spring of 1907, a fire was discovered in the Sing Kew Theatre on Shanghai Alley. The fire was thought to have been

set deliberately in an attempt to burn down Chinatown. On September 7 of the same year, the Asiatic Exclusion League held a meeting in Vancouver's old city hall. League members wanted to get rid of British Columbia's oriental immigrants, and inflammatory racist speeches aroused the crowd to such a pitch that they burst out of the building and swept through Chinatown. The mob smashed windows and whatever else presented an easy target. By the time they reached the Japanese quarter, the residents had had time to grab bottles and clubs to defend their property.

The riot was soon over, but while injuries were not reported, several thousand dollars' worth of damage had been done. The Chinese demanded compensation, and the federal government sent the deputy minister of labour, William Lyon Mackenzie King, to assess the damage. King recommended payment of some $27,000 to cover damages and legal expenses.

The racially motivated violence and claims for damages had other unanticipated consequences. Among the claims were two from opium factories, each claiming $500 for loss of income. King was horrified to discover that it was legal to make and sell opium and that drug use was spreading to the white community. Back in Ottawa, he introduced a bill in Parliament to deal with the problem; the first Opium and Narcotic Drug Act was introduced in Canada in 1929.

While that act put the Vancouver opium factories out of

business, it merely meant that drug users and suppliers had to hide their activities. As police grew more efficient at catching smugglers who came ashore with bulky packages of opium, smugglers grew more inventive. Ships entering the harbour began to drop their cargo of opium overboard, sealed in waterproof cans. The cans were retrieved later by small boats, when no one was paying attention. Sometimes the opium packages were tied to the end of a long line weighted with a lump of lead, and sometimes the opium was tied to a bladder buoy weighted with a block of salt. Over several days, the salt slowly dissolved and allowed the buoy to float to the surface of the sea; again, it would be retrieved by a small boat that didn't attract attention. To try to end the smuggling, the police force acquired its first boat in 1911, but the opium smugglers often outwitted police, and the number of addicts rose. Eventually they switched to heroin, a derivative of opium.

The racial violence in 1907 also led to more exclusionary measures being incorporated into a new Canadian immigration law that was put into effect in 1910.

Frugality and Philanthropy

By 1908, the Wing Sang Company was one of the largest Chinese companies in Vancouver. Its import-export business alone brought in $50,000 a year, and its real-estate holdings were estimated to be worth over $200,000. The Yip family members were well provided for, but Yip Sang was frugal and kept a tight control over his money. Despite his

Yip Sang (fifth from left) with other family members in front of the newly extended Wing Sang Company Building in 1902. CITY OF VANCOUVER ARCHIVES 689-54

parsimonious nature, he passed on this piece of advice to his son Dock: "When you in business, don't do it cheap. Charge high fee or you wasting your time." He similarly believed that if something was worth doing, it was worth doing well. He continued to invest in business opportunities, but he now had the wherewithal to consider not only financial investments but also those that enhanced the quality of life of those less fortunate than himself.

Medical staff at the Vancouver General Hospital would not treat patients of Chinese origin; however, the hospital needed more facilities to accommodate Vancouver's expanding population. Yip Sang donated money toward a new building on the condition that Chinese patients would be treated there in future, and he also joined the hospital board as a lifetime governor. He helped to establish the Mount St. Joseph Oriental Hospital, where Missionary Sisters of the Immaculate Conception cared for tuberculosis patients as well as a group of elderly homeless men. Not forgetting his roots, Yip Sang donated money to the Guangdong Public Hospital in Guangzhou and was a major benefactor for the Taishan No. 1 Middle School, built in 1909.

Chaos in China

Like other immigrants, the Chinese avidly followed their homeland politics. Those in Canada either wanted to return to China with enough money to live a decent life in peace or to stay in Canada, have their families join them and be treated like other Canadians. Whatever their dream, they especially wanted to see China strengthened in the global arena, hoping that racism in Canada would lessen if China became a respected power. What's more, Canada's immigration policies were affected by international power struggles. If China could stabilize her political situation and improve her economy, then perhaps her emigrants would be treated with more respect.

The failure of the Boxer Rebellion in China was enough to make even conservative or old-fashioned members of the Qing elite realize that they would have to accept reforms in order to survive. They began to make changes to help them move from an absolute monarchy to a constitutional one. They reinstated some of the earlier reforms and got rid of the exclusionary imperial examination system, by which educated men could become governors, that had been in place since 1380. People were looking for radical solutions, believing that the Manchus' insistence upon tradition was partly responsible for China's difficulties.

Dr. Sun Yat-sen, a medical graduate from a college in Hong Kong, believed he had the answer to China's woes. Frustrated by the Qing government's reluctance to move with the times, he gave up medicine and turned to politics. During his time in Hong Kong, and also in Hawaii, he had been exposed to western ideas and believed that China needed to abandon the imperial system and become a republic. China had been governed for too long by men who lived in opulence while the ordinary people starved. Dr. Sun Yat-sen believed that elected representatives should govern the country, thus creating a government of the people, by the people, for the people. During the 1890s, his ideas became increasingly popular. His revolutionaries become known as the Chinese Nationalist Party, or the Guomindang (Kuomintang). He began to travel through China, and then increasingly outside the country, spreading his ideas and raising money to support revolutionary activities. These activities included uprisings against Qing governors, but none succeeded, and he was exiled from China after one such failure in 1895.

Dr. Sun Yat-sen continued to visit overseas Chinese communities, and in 1897 made a successful visit to Vancouver and Victoria, where most of Canada's Chinese population lived. When he returned to Canada in 1910 and 1911, he included eastern Canada in his itinerary. The Chinese communities, and particularly members of the Chinese Freemasons Society, responded to the doctor's ideas with interest and enthusiasm, and by his third visit to Vancouver his daily lectures in the Sing Kew Theatre in Shanghai Alley were packed. Supporters hoped the Guomindang would reverse China's fortunes, and they contributed generously to the cause. Some even took out mortgages on buildings they owned, and their contributions added up to thousands of dollars.

Emperor Guangxu died under suspicious circumstances on November 14, 1908. The 73-year-old Dowager Empress Cixi, who was very ill by this time, died the following day. She had named Puyi as China's next emperor, but since he was not quite three years old when Emperor Guangxu died, regents were appointed to rule in Puyi's place until he came of age. These regents, once again chosen from the Qing elite, slowed down the reform process.

While Dr. Sun Yat-sen was exiled, the Guomindang, in

another coup, took control of the capital of Hubei Province, now called Wuhan, on October 10, 1911. This was the beginning of the end of the faltering Qing Dynasty. The doctor returned to China to become provisional president while elections were organized. The delicate task of obtaining the emperor's abdication was given to Yuan Shikai, a powerful general in the Qing regime's imperial army with connections to both the Qing governors and ex-imperial army soldiers who had joined the revolutionary army. Puyi was allowed to live on in the Forbidden City with the title of emperor, but he was stripped of his imperial powers. As a negotiated reward for making this arrangement, Yuan Shikai was installed as the first president of the new regime.

It took time to remove a centuries-old system of government. While the new system was being put in place, Yuan Shikai named himself president for life. By 1916, he was trying to establish a new imperial dynasty with himself as emperor. When the people refused to accept this, Yuan Shikai fled, and without another strong and charismatic figure to take his place, the country fell apart. Warlords grabbed power, and for the next decade or so there was no effective government in China.

CHAPTER

Expansion
and Restrictions

IN 1912, YIP SANG BUILT a new six-storey brick building behind the Wing Sang building. The two were connected by a narrow corridor at ground level and an enclosed passageway on the third floor. In the intervening years, Yip Sang's wives had blessed him with 19 sons and 4 daughters, and the original building must have been bursting at the seams.

The grandmothers and their families moved onto different floors of the building. Number One Grandmother, Dong Shee, lived on the third floor of the three-storey building. Number Three Grandmother, Chin Shee, lived on the fifth floor of the six-storey addition with the rest of her family, while Number Two Grandmother, Wong Shee, and her family occupied the sixth floor. The stairways were long and steep, but even with their bound feet, the grandmothers were able to nip up and down with surprising speed when necessary.

The second floor of the new building had rows of bunks occupied by new immigrants looking for work. The first floor housed a kitchen where meals were cooked for all the male Yips and any other men staying there. At 5 PM, diners were summoned with a handbell to simple meals that mostly consisted of steamed rice, vegetables stir-fried in three huge woks, and perhaps some chicken or salt fish. The women and children ate in their apartments upstairs, but there were live-in maids to help cook the meals.

There was always a bed and an extra set of chopsticks for a newly arrived immigrant or someone out of work. Other members of the community said that Yip Sang was going to go broke because of this, but those free meals and bunk beds generated a lot of good will. He sometimes even provided a start-up loan to a new immigrant without asking for collateral or a promissory note. Yip Sang never reneged on a deal, and he didn't expect other people to do so either.

The third floor of the original three-storey building housed a classroom. Although Yip Sang had no formal schooling, Confucian values such as self-improvement were ingrained in him, and he recognized the value of education. Book learning allowed men to rise above their humble origins, and for over 500 years it had been the process of studying and passing the imperial examinations that allowed men to become part of the administrative elite, or *shi*, in China. On the day his grandson Sun Wing Yip started school, Yip Sang sat the boy on his lap and told him to study hard and learn as much as he could. A provincial law requiring all children to be in school between the ages of 7 and 15 was not passed until 1921, however Yip Sang's children had all attended school and some had gone on to university, including at least one of his daughters. This was unusual in the 1920s, when many parents thought that a university education was wasted on a girl who would probably marry and spend her days running a home and caring for children.

Yip Sang's children attended public school because he thought it was important for them to interact with the non-Chinese community. However, he hired private tutors from China and Hong Kong, who visited on student visas, to teach them Chinese. Neighbours' children were invited to attend these lessons as well. Yip Sang also sponsored the Oy Kuo Night School for adults and was its principal for 10 years. The schoolroom had two rows of tables and chairs, with chalkboards along one wall and the family's ancestor altar along another wall. When the tables and chairs were pushed aside, the large room was a perfect place to hold meetings and parties.

Yip Sang in 1920, aged 74 or 75.
CITY OF VANCOUVER ARCHIVES 689-129

The Ancestor Altar

Confucius taught that it was important to respect and honour family elders and ancestors, and one way to show such respect was by assembling an ancestor altar. Yip Sang's altar was made from two tables, one tall and narrow with a shorter, square one protruding at right angles from beneath the taller one. The taller table, imported from China and decorated with appropriate carvings, held candles, vases of flowers and a bronze burner filled with sand and ash that held burning sticks of incense. The altar held Lee Shee's soul tablet, a portable memorial that rested on a support with carved legs. Also on the tables and the wall behind them were photos, which in later years included those of Yip Sang and his other three wives.

On special days, such as an ancestor's birthday or the anniversary of their death, the altar was decorated with flowers and burning incense. An offering to the ancestors to come and eat was placed on the altar. This offering was often a boiled chicken or barbequed pork and three shot glasses containing whisky, along with three pairs of chopsticks. Family members would bow to each ancestor portrait and later eat the chicken or pork. If no one drank the whisky, it was poured back into the bottle, although Yip Sang and his sons enjoyed a tot or two of whisky on occasion. Long after his death, Yip Sang's portrait commanded a place of honour at the altar on birthdays, weddings and religious holidays.

Colleagues and Competitors

With all the discriminatory regulations and animosity they faced, it was difficult for Chinese Canadians to flourish as they switched back and forth between mainstream society and the sanctity of the Chinese community. One such regulation particularly affected Chinese restaurants. In 1912, provinces began to ban Chinese businesses from hiring white women, who often worked as waitresses, in an attempt to reduce interracial contact. But despite such obstacles, a few other Chinese men besides Yip Sang were able to make names for themselves.

Won Alexander Cumyow was born in Port Douglas at the head of Harrison Lake in 1861. He was the first known baby of Chinese descent born in Canada and was duly registered as a British subject. Port Douglas was at the start of the Douglas Trail to Lillooet, constructed for the flow of goods and miners to the Fraser River gold rush. Rock piles can still be seen along the Fraser River at Lillooet, below Hangman's Tree Park and downstream from the old suspension bridge. Chinese prospectors piled these washed stones in long rows that reached more than 3.5 metres high in places.

Won Alexander Cumyow's father, Won Ling Sing, had emigrated from Guangdong to San Francisco in 1858, just six years before Yip Sang. Won Ling Sing and his wife ran a restaurant and a store that sold clothing and equipment to gold prospectors. Some of their customers were First Nations peoples, who taught Won Alexander Cumyow to speak Chinook Jargon, a pidgin trade language used by First Nations peoples to communicate with other First Nations groups or non-Aboriginals.

Business dropped off as the Cariboo Wagon Road became the more popular route into the interior, and in the early

1870s, the Won family moved to New Westminster, where the children attended school. After he had completed school, Won Alexander Cumyow became a bookkeeper and worked in his father's stores. He later moved to Victoria, where he studied law, but by this time, Chinese Canadians were not allowed to vote. This had serious repercussions for those aspiring to certain professions, including law, accounting, engineering, pharmacy and medicine. When they obtained their degrees, graduates had to join the appropriate professional organization in order to practise their occupation, but to obtain certification by these organizations, their names had to be included on the list of eligible voters. While this requirement was presumably set in place to ensure that only legitimate professionals legally entitled to live in the province could practise, it meant that anyone who was denied the vote was also denied the ability to work in their chosen profession. Unable to practise law, Won Alexander Cumyow became a court interpreter for the Vancouver police, where he made good use of his knowledge of Cantonese, another Chinese dialect called Hakka and Chinook Jargon.

Won Alexander Cumyow married and fathered 10 children, but he still found time for endless business and community activities, including serving as spokesman for the Chinese community. He was also secretary for the Vancouver branch of the Chinese Empire Reform Association (Yip Sang was president). This political party was established by Kang Youwei, who wanted to establish a constitutional monarchy in China. Won Alexander Cumyow also worked to have the vote restored to Chinese Canadians. He lived long enough to see this happen after the Second World War, when Chinese Canadians were allowed to vote in the 1949 federal election. Many photographs were taken of him casting his vote. When he retired, his third son, Gordon, took over his position of court interpreter. Won Alexander Cumyow died in 1955 at the age of 94. His son, Gordon, became the first Chinese notary public in Canada.

Chang Toy was another successful Chinese businessman, even though he never did learn to speak much English. Born in Guangdong Province in 1857, he left his wife in China and travelled to British Columbia in 1874, where he worked as a contract labourer. He worked brief stints in a fish cannery to repay his passage money and at a sawmill before buying an interest in a Chinese laundry that also sold groceries. Later, he bought out his partner. The store brought him into contact with labourers looking for work, and he began contracting their labour to salmon canneries and land-clearing operations. Like Yip Sang and other Chinese entrepreneurs, he kept an eye open for opportunities to make money.

One such opportunity arose because land was being cleared for development and a large amount of wood was available. Charcoal could be made by burning dry wood for several days in a hole in the ground, or in an airless, earth-covered mound, and it had many domestic and commercial uses at the time. It burns at a high temperature, so was used in blast furnaces for iron manufacturing, and it could be easily transported by rail. Chang Toy began to operate charcoal burners and sell the charcoal.

In 1888, Chang Toy established the Sam Kee Company, which became one of the Wing Sang Company's greatest competitors. With a gross annual income of around $165,000, the Sam Kee Company was one of the four highest-earning companies in Vancouver's Chinatown. The company continued to manufacture charcoal and to contract labour to shingle mills, canneries and sugar-beet farms. It operated a herring saltery in Nanaimo, imported and exported food products to and from China and served as agents for the Blue Funnel Steamship Line, a rival of the CPR ships on the trans-Pacific route. Chang Toy also bought lots and buildings both inside and outside Vancouver's Chinatown. These eventually included waterfront property and several residential hotels.

After the anti-Asian riot of September 7, 1907, Chang Toy and his business partner marched down to a gun merchant, bought all of the revolvers and shared them out among the local merchants. But perhaps this pioneer is best known for the Sam Kee building on 8 West Pender Street. Like the Wing Sang Company building, it has been named a heritage building to be preserved as a significant part of Vancouver's history. The lot it stands on was standard-sized when Chang Toy bought it in 1903, but in 1912 the city wanted to widen Pender Street. They expropriated 7.3 metres of the lot, leaving Chang Toy with only 1.8 metres. Many people would consider this narrow space unusable, but Chang Toy had not been compensated for this portion of his property and, determined not to waste a valuable piece of land, he had a building specially designed to fit on the lot. The basement extended beneath the sidewalk and originally housed public baths and a barber shop, while the main floor consisted of offices and shops. The second storey, widened slightly by projecting bay windows, was used for living quarters. For a while, the Guinness Book of Records listed the building as the thinnest commercial building in the world, but this has since been challenged by buildings in Pittsburgh and Philadelphia, which are thinner but not freestanding.

There were a handful of other successful and wealthy merchants in Vancouver and Victoria, and the owners of the opium factories made good money while they were operating, but these were the exceptions to the large bachelor communities of impoverished Chinese labourers.

Discipline
Yip Sang wanted the best of both worlds for his family. He felt that it was important for them to take part in the traditions of their new homeland. He also instilled in them the traditions and beliefs he brought with him from China. It was not customary for Chinese fathers to show a lot of emotion toward their children, and Yip Sang was a strict authoritarian, but this was probably necessary in a household with 23 children.

No doubt their hijinks could have got out of hand at times without a parent, or four parents in this case, keeping a close eye on what was going on.

As the youngsters grew old enough to go out on their own, Yip Sang set a 10 PM curfew. He said that all the businesses were closed by 6 PM, so this gave members of his household plenty of time to do whatever they wanted. He kept the only keys to the building's door and locked it at 10 PM every evening. Of course, the youngsters sometimes stayed out later anyway and climbed the fire escape to get back in. One evening, a policeman caught sight of one of the boys and asked what he was doing. The boy explained that he lived there but had been locked out. The policeman allowed him to continue on up but reported him to Yip Sang the next day. The game was over, although it's highly likely their father already knew how they got in after hours. With so many people living together, there were few secrets.

Yip Sang used a cane on his sons, but not his daughters, if he thought they deserved it, a punishment that was not unusual in those days. One of his sons, Yip Kew Dock, described him as a hard but good man, knowing that this sounded like an oxymoron. Yip Sang never looked down on anyone. He was hardworking, honest and took pride in his family.

Mounting Unrest

Even though established families, like the Yips and Wons, showed themselves to be responsible citizens, this did not allay the fears of the non-Chinese population. Tension between different ethnic groups resulted in clashes, such as the 1907 Vancouver riot, and the concerned Canadian government worked to impose more restrictions on immigrants who did not assimilate into the general population. They entered into negotiations with foreign nations to restrict the departure of their nationals and introduced a new immigration law in 1910. This new law allowed the federal cabinet discretionary power to regulate the admission of immigrants to Canada. To avoid the drain that destitute immigrants placed on the country's resources, a $25 head tax was introduced for all immigrants who were not already subject to one. Immigrants could also be deported for moral or political reasons. To make it harder for potential immigrants to evade restrictions put in place by their own governments, new immigrants to Canada were allowed to enter the country only if they had travelled by one continuous journey from the country in which they were either born or had acquired nationality, or through tickets purchased before leaving their country of origin. These new regulations also enabled authorities to deny entry to immigrants from Asia who did not have $200 in cash on their person. These last two regulations affected not only the Chinese, but also immigrants from countries such as India, as was evident in the infamous *Komagatu Maru* incident in 1914, where 376 East Indian immigrants were denied entry to Canada.

CHAPTER

7

The First Canadian-Born Generation

OVER THE YEARS, YIP SANG acquired shares in assorted companies and properties such as the Hotel West. His sons helped to run some of his businesses, including Sonny's Marketeria, Shanghai Service Station and the Sang Remittance Company, and were paid very modest salaries.

Yip Kew Lap, Yip Sang's thirteenth son, was a pilot-navigator on one of the saltery boats. Yip Sang assigned an accountant to each herring saltery and, eventually, one of his sons as on-site manager. Yip Sang's tenth son, Yip Kew Dang, managed the saltery on Galiano Island. It was a seasonal business that closed during the winter. His family didn't see much of him during the rest of the year, but when his children and some of their cousins were old enough to occupy themselves without supervision they spent school summer holidays on the island and slept in the saltery bunkhouse.

Instead of a salary, Yip Sang provided food and accommodation, and the families took whatever clothes and shoes they needed from the store. When Dang pointed out that his employees earned more than he did and asked for some spending money, Yip Sang refused, saying he provided everything Dang and his wife and children needed. What did he need money for? He would get his share of the family money eventually. They didn't know that he would never inherit any of his father's fortune. Despite the fact that his sons were on site and in charge, Yip Sang received a daily telephone report on the operations of his salteries and made any necessary decisions. Occasionally, he took a grandson with him to inspect the plants. He retained overall control of these salteries until his death.

Dang wasn't the only son who wanted some spending money. Yip Sang's eighth son, Yip Kew Park, had already been matched with a wife and was engaged. When he went to Hong Kong to marry his fiancée, his brothers Sheck (the ninth son) and Dang decided to accompany him. They asked their father for money, but Yip Sang said that if they wanted spending money, they would also have to marry. While they were in Hong Kong, Park's fiancée introduced them to suitable marriage partners who also happened to be her old school friends. The three sons were married in birth order in February, March and April of the same year. Having the company of two longtime friends no doubt helped the three brides settle into their new home and large family. The name Dang sounded like the Cantonese word for oranges, so when his children came along, Dang called them his little oranges.

Yip Kew Sheck, Ming and Yacht, Yip Sang's ninth, fourteenth and nineteenth sons, ran the remittance company that transferred customers' savings back to China. Yip Kew Dang and Yacht also ran the Shanghai Service gas station. Fifth son Yip Kew Him was a director of Kue Hing Co. and ran a bake shop called Canada Cafe. He also worked as an interpreter. In 1916, he charged $3 a day or $1.50 for half a day. By 1930, this had increased to $10 a day.

With 23 children, it was inevitable that some of them would be athletic, but one in particular made a name for himself—Yip Sang's sixteenth son, Yip Kew Quene. While attending King George High School, Quene won the individual championship at the 1925 Vancouver Inter-High School track and field meet. He also excelled at soccer and was known for his dazzling footwork. He continued with both track and field and soccer during his single year of study at the University of British Columbia (UBC) and was varsity star centre forward both at UBC and at Queen's University, where he attended from 1927 to 1929. But he is perhaps best known for his play on a soccer team formed by Vancouver's Chinese Students Athletic Association in 1920. The team began with a group of friends playing in

Chinatown. Yip Sang said his sons were wasting their time playing soccer when they could be earning money, but they played anyway. At first, they didn't have a coach. They learned by watching other teams and practised with a tennis ball. They didn't have anyone to play against either, until their sponsor, a Chinatown bank, entered them into a league. However, the team of high-school students was mistakenly entered in the city's adult league. They played on Wednesday nights against firemen, policemen and other players who were often larger and stronger.

Their team reached its zenith in 1933 when it beat UBC's Blue and Gold varsity squad in the final match of the prestigious open knockout tournament known as the BC Mainland Cup. The Chinese students had refused to be drawn into the rough or dirty tactics sometimes demonstrated by opposing teams and had won cleanly. The mostly white members of the press spoke of Quene's speed and mental agility, his brother Art's nimble passes and goaltender Shupon "Spoon" Wong's catlike speed. This came at a time when Canadians of Chinese origin were not only burdened by the widespread economic depression but also referred to as "the chinks" in a UBC newsletter and expected to sit in a roped-off section of the cinema and give way to white people on sidewalks. In need of something they could feel proud about, Chinatown went wild. There are reports that the triumphant victory parade was phoned in to the police as a suspected riot and that exploding firecrackers set off a fire alarm, causing two fire trucks to arrive. The next day was declared to be a holiday with free tea and dim sum for everyone. Quene Yip was inducted into the BC Sports Hall of Fame in 1998, and in 2011 the entire team, which included Quene's brothers Dock and Art, was inducted.

For a while, Quene took over management of the saltery on the west shore of Saltery Bay, Galiano Island, which his father had established in 1913, from his brother Mow. He went on to become a chemist and worked for the Pacific Lime Company in Blubber Bay on Texada Island. He also worked as an agent for Sun Life Insurance Company. Not surprisingly, business was slow during the Depression years, so Quene and his wife, Victoria, would listen to news of the war on the radio, write it up in Chinese and post it on a noticeboard.

Despite the challenge of passing junior matriculation exams without having much knowledge of western ideologies, such as the Bible, and having to study in a language they only spoke at school, Quene wasn't the only one of Yip Sang's children to go on to university. His fourth daughter, Yip Gim Ling, or Susan, also studied at UBC and then Columbia University in New York. At Columbia, she met her husband, who was a student from China. After completing a master's degree in 1922, Susan moved with her husband to China, where she worked as a translator for the Chinese government, then as principal of a girls' school in Guangdong and later as a professor of English at

Sun Yat-sen University in Guangzhou. Susan returned to live in Canada when she retired.

Yip Kew Ghim, Yip Sang's eleventh son, graduated from medical school at Queen's University in the late 1920s. Although he was restricted to working in Chinatown, he practised both western and Chinese medicine and was no doubt instrumental in helping to break down the mistrust his Chinese patients had for western treatments. In those days, patients either paid for medical care or went without, but in 1928, Dr. Yip established a free weekly health clinic in Vancouver's Chinatown for the elderly or others who couldn't afford to pay. Family members were treated with no charge for either his services or the drugs he prescribed. Dr. Yip also helped to run Mount Saint Joseph Oriental Hospital (St. Joseph's), campaigned to raise funds to construct a new St. Joseph's and served on the board of directors for many years. He didn't drive or own a car, but as his patients were all in Chinatown, everything was within walking distance.

In their earlier years, Art, the eighteenth son, and Dock, the seventeenth son, worked on the boats *Yip 1* and *Yip 2*, which delivered fish to the cannery. Dock moved to New York City in 1928 to attend Columbia University, where he had the idea of starting up a pharmacy business with a group of fellow students after graduation. He worked as a waiter in a chop-suey house to help pay his student fees, but was appalled by the behaviour of the white customers who "perform all sorts of immoral actions in the restaurants" and "spend all their wages on prostitution, extravagance and dissipations of every sort." The only reason he worked there was because a good waiter could earn as much as $250 a month. He also found New York to be dangerous and wrote to his older brother Mow about the tong wars: "It is terrible in New York, especially Chinatown. I don't go there and have never been out late. It is too risky in New York— too many hold ups." Disillusioned with New York, Dock transferred to Michigan University, but lack of money was a continual problem, and during the summer of 1929, he took on a "hellish" job as advertising manager in Chicago. Despite a tendency to become distracted by extracurricular activities, Dock graduated from the University of Michigan with a degree in pharmacy in 1931.

By this time, however, Dock realized that he was better at speaking than using his hands and decided he would rather become a lawyer. Since Osgoode Hall Law School didn't recognize American degrees, he took a bachelor of arts degree at UBC. By this time, the Yip family fortune had taken a turn for the worse, and he needed to work. He found a job at the Chinese consulate, and schooling was relegated to after-work hours. Dock graduated from UBC in 1941, married his childhood sweetheart, Victoria Chow, joined the Queen's Own Rifles as a reservist and the following year moved to Toronto and began his law program. While studying at Osgoode Hall, he teamed up with a fellow law student named Irving Himmel to form a committee to repeal the

Chinese Immigration Act. The two continued this work after they graduated and were key players in the team that went to Ottawa to petition the government to repeal the act in 1947.

Like his father, Dock was a strong believer in education and helping those less fortunate. In the evenings, he turned his law office into a school where new immigrants could learn English, law, accounting and ballroom dancing. He also served two terms as a school trustee in Toronto. When he retired, he tried his hand at acting, and in 1985 his Chinese accent helped him to land a speaking part in the Hollywood movie *Year of the Dragon*.

A man of many talents, Dock is best remembered for his work as Canada's first Chinese-Canadian lawyer. When asked during his student days why he was attending law school when Chinese people were not allowed to practise law in Canada, he replied, "Yes, that is true, but I am a Canadian."

Coming from a young man whose family and friends were asked to use the back entrance to the hotel where a family celebration was being held, this statement shows the determination he carried through life.

The First World War

As a dominion of Britain, Canada was automatically at war when Britain declared war on Germany on August 4, 1914. Recruiting for the Canadian army was done on a volunteer basis at first, and the Canadian government called for 20,000 volunteers. In less than a month, 40,000 men had volunteered. Recruits of Chinese origin who were either naturalized citizens or had been born in Canada were refused in British Columbia and had to travel to other provinces if they wanted to enlist. Conscription was introduced in August 1917, when voluntary enlistment was not raising sufficient troops; however, men of Chinese origin were not conscripted either. As a result, very few fought in the First World War, although a small number volunteered and served in the infantry.

Labourers from China were recruited into the Chinese Labour Corps, however, when the government of China declared war on Germany and Austria in 1917. Allied casualties during the Battle of the Somme were horrendous, and labourers were desperately needed. About 50,000 men were recruited from Shandong Province and transported across Canada in sealed railway cars on their way to France. Although they were not sent within 16 kilometres of the front line, their camps were sometimes under fire from long-range shelling or strafing. The Chinese men maintained machines and vehicles, loaded and unloaded supplies from trains and ships, built roads, dug trenches and helped clean up the battlefields. When the war ended, they were quarantined at William Head on Vancouver Island to await their ship back to Asia. A riot broke out in March 1919, and about 2,000 of these labourers broke out of confinement. Most were rounded up and sent back to China, but some found refuge in Victoria's Chinatown.

The war brought fuel and food shortages that led to rationing of everyday items. Farm labourers were scarce, and food was being sent to Britain and, later in the war, by the Canadian Red Cross to Canadian prisoners of war. Medical equipment and personnel were shipped across the Atlantic along with other items, including over 60 million shells for guns. The drain on Canada's finite resources was huge. Limited in the number of ways that it could generate revenue, the government raised import tariffs, introduced new taxes and issued national war bonds.

Personal income tax, like other wartime taxes, began as a temporary measure. Canada's gross national debt soared from $544 million in 1914 to almost $2.5 billion in 1919, with most of this money raised in Canada itself through public war loans. Vancouver's Chinese Canadians helped the war effort by buying $100,000 worth of war bonds, which became known as Victory Bonds after 1917. These raised money to finance military operations.

When the war ended in 1918, public gatherings were banned and public buildings closed—the returning soldiers had brought a different kind of enemy home with them. It was called the Spanish influenza. People wore surgical masks in an attempt to limit their exposure to airborne microbes, but despite these precautions, the epidemic in the fall of 1918 killed 50,000 Canadians.

As if this wasn't bad enough, Vancouver's economic boom had collapsed. Real-estate prices that had soared between 1908 and 1912 began to fall in 1913. It would be 1950 before land prices reached 1912 levels again. Homeowners were left with large mortgages they couldn't pay on property they couldn't sell.

The Chinese Immigration Act

After the war, it became clear that the number of Asians in Canada was still increasing and, fuelled by job shortages and financial difficulties, hostility towards Asian immigrants continued to escalate. As a result, a new Chinese Immigration Act was passed by Parliament in 1923. Although it did away with the head taxes, it became known in the Chinese-Canadian community as the Chinese Exclusion Act because it banned all Chinese immigrants from entering Canada except for those classified as merchants, diplomats, foreign students and a few with special circumstances. This affected many families and the Louie family in particular. Mrs. Louie was visiting family in China when the act came into effect and wasn't allowed to return to her husband and children in Canada. It was 15 years before 13-year-old Alex Louie and his brothers saw their mother again.

The act required all Chinese people living in Canada, even those born in Canada, to register with the government so they could be issued a certificate of registration. It came into effect on July 1, 1923—Dominion Day. Canadians of Chinese origin called it the Day of Humiliation and refused to celebrate Canada Day for years afterwards. Some wore badges with the phrases "the Chinese are being treated unfairly" or "human rights are being violated" in Chinese characters. The Japanese were treated similarly. In 1928, Japanese officials agreed to allow no more than 150 of their citizens to immigrate to Canada. They also agreed not to allow any more picture brides. These were women who travelled to Canada to marry Canadians of Japanese origin whom they had never met before.

However, by the mid-1920s, the nation was booming and more working people were needed. Thousands of immigrants from central and eastern Europe were admitted to Canada through various agreements over the following years. While some worried that English-speaking farmers were gradually being replaced by central Europeans, and communism was seen as a threat to democratic government and the Canadian way of life, this immigration continued until the start of the Depression.

The Death of the Patriarch

Yip Sang's 60th, 70th and 80th birthdays were marked with the help of many friends and relatives. By the last year of his life, Yip Sang had a bleeding ulcer and couldn't walk down the five flights of stairs to the store. He still liked to sit and greet customers and watch what was going on, so two of his sons would carry him down flights of stairs from his room and settle him in his big black leather chair. Yip Sang died on July 20, 1927, at the age of 81.

IN MEMORIAM
YIP SANG
1845 – 1927
"AT REST"

先考諱連生字來餞號春田黃公墓

廣東省台山縣都斛望頭村
生于前清道光廿四年九月初六日丑時
歿于中華民國十六年七月二十日午時
享壽八十有二歲

YIP SANG

Having made Canada his home, Yip Sang requested
that his remains not be shipped back to China.
He was buried in Vancouver's Mountain View
Cemetery. FRANCES HERN

Chiang Kai-Shek, leader of the Nationalist Party in
China, sent a message of condolence, but it wasn't only
Chinese who mourned "Uncle" Sang. He'd believed in
integration, despite the fact that Chinese Canadians were
still considered a separate class and tended to keep to themselves, and he had many non-Chinese friends.

Yip Sang's funeral procession began at the funeral parlour on Beatty Street. His grandson, Sun Wing Yip, remembers walking behind the hearse as a 10-year-old with his parents and uncles, dressed in a white shirt and black armband. The women all wore white. Rows of mourners followed in both western suits and oriental dress, with over a hundred cars—likely half the cars in Vancouver at the time—and a marching band. The hearse stopped outside the Wing Sang Company building, the casket was opened and Pastor Kwan, the Methodist minister, conducted the service right there before continuing on to the cemetery.

In his last will and testament, Yip Sang left $100 to each of his two oldest sons, Yip Kew Yow and Yip Kew Suey. Traditionally, Chinese daughters were not bequeathed any of their father's property because they were expected to marry into another family. After expenses, the remainder of his estate was distributed equally between all his male children, with the oldest male child from each of wives number two, three and four taking charge of their portion of the family's money.

The Depression

Yip Sang's children and grandchildren must have missed his guidance during the difficult times that followed his death. Canada's economy had grown rapidly through the 1920s, and companies expanded during this boom time, eager to increase profits. Canadians bought real estate and stocks with borrowed money. Americans were investing heavily in stocks too. In October 1929, prices on the New York Stock Exchange began to falter for the first time in several years. Periods of selling and high volumes of trading were interspersed with brief periods of rising prices and recovery, so prices began to seesaw. Worried investors began to sell. On October 29, 1929—a day known as Black Tuesday—prices plummeted. The market lost $14 billion in one day.

As the crash continued, investors lost their money, companies went bankrupt and real-estate values plummeted. The United States sank into an economic depression that spread around the world. Britain was badly affected too, and because Britain and the United States were Canada's main trading partners, demand for Canadian natural resources dropped. Companies that had expanded found themselves with higher expenses and lower cash flow. Employees were let go or had their wages reduced to the absolute minimum. Personal belongings bought on credit were repossessed, and people were evicted from their homes. There was no welfare as we know it today.

To make matters worse, a bad year for prairie farmers turned into a prolonged drought that became known as the Dirty Thirties. The lack of rain combined with poor soil-conservation techniques to create a dust bowl. Dust storms that obscured vision and coated everything with grit began in 1931. Farmers couldn't grow crops or feed their livestock. They couldn't feed their families either, and many simply walked away from their farms.

Unemployment reached 27 percent in 1933, with a quarter of Canada's population unable to find work. The Conservative prime minister, Richard Bedford Bennett, insisted that caring for the jobless was primarily a local and provincial responsibility. However, he agreed to the creation of camps for homeless, single males, set up through the Department of National Defence. In exchange for a bed in a bunkhouse, three meals a day, work clothes, medical care and 20 cents a day, these "Royal Twenty Centers" worked 44 hours a week clearing bush, constructing roads and public buildings, and planting trees. By 1932, there were over 8,000 men working in these camps.

People were desperate for work and the means to feed themselves and their families. Some committed suicide. Some protested and demonstrated. Some simply starved. Non-British immigrants who had lived in Canada for less than five years, or British immigrants who had lived in Canada for less than one year could be deported if they were unemployed or "got into trouble." This vague phrase could encompass union activities, membership in the Communist Party, health problems or minor criminal charges such as vagrancy. The only immigrants allowed into Canada during these difficult years were farmers able to support themselves, immediate relatives of Canadian residents, and British subjects and Americans who had enough capital to support themselves until the job market improved. Between 1930 and 1934, over 16,000 immigrants were deported from Canada for becoming a public charge. Thousands of desperate men from colder parts of Canada rode the rails to Vancouver, where at least they wouldn't freeze to death. They congregated around False Creek and the Burrard Inlet railyards, creating hobo jungles. City authorities feared both typhoid and the spread of communism and regularly burned these clusters of makeshift dwellings to the ground. As the weather improved, more workers deserted the relief camps and rebuilt the jungles.

None of this helped attitudes toward Chinese Canadians. Some people agitated against them and also asked for Chinese business licences to be revoked. The authorities said this would be discriminatory and illegal, but opposition to Chinese businesses continued into the 1940s. Their own support groups could only do so much, and some Chinese were forced to apply for relief, a humiliating experience. In British Columbia, the relief allowance for a single Chinese-Canadian man was $1.72. In Alberta it was $1.12. This was less than half of what was given to a single non-Chinese man, but officials justified it by claiming that the Chinese standard of living was lower so they could manage with less. Sixty-three Chinese Canadians were cut off relief in Calgary after it was reported that the Chinese community had donated $10,000 to support China in its war against Japan. Officials felt that if they could afford to send money overseas, they didn't need relief.

Canada's economy eventually recovered, but the challenges faced by the Chinese community were far from over.

The Second Canadian-Born Generation

BETWEEN 1902 AND 1948, Yip Sang's children produced 81 grandchildren. Yip Sang didn't live long enough to meet them all, but for years his home reverberated with all the activities engaged in by cousins of varying ages. There was always someone to play with, and companions provided protection too. An individual accompanied by a couple of siblings or cousins was less likely to be picked on and teased or beaten up, as sometimes happened with Chinese children, and even adults, when they ventured beyond Chinatown.

The Yip household even had enough players to make up teams. In the 1940s, there was very little traffic along Chinatown's Columbia Street, and on Sundays some of the cousins played hockey on roller skates, stopping to move their homemade nets out of the way if a car approached. They also had a basketball hoop on the sundeck off the third floor. Naturally, the play grew boisterous at times, especially when bad weather forced the youngsters indoors. The third-floor grand hall was large enough for soccer and roller hockey, but one day Number Fifteen Uncle, who had the misfortune to live in the rooms at the end of the hall and had to rise early for his shift with a fruit and vegetable wholesaler, lost patience with all the thumps and bangs as players roller skated into the adjoining wall. After one thump too many, he hammered in nails so that they protruded into the grand hall. Players skating into the wall now risked impaling themselves.

Another time, an older cousin with a bedroom directly beneath the schoolroom, who worked a night shift, took an axe to the Ping-Pong table in the schoolroom so he could get some sleep. The schoolroom had windows with long curtains that the younger children hid behind when playing hide-and-seek. They also liked to pull empty rice sacks, made of bamboo fibre, up over their legs and slide down the flights of stairs.

Luckily, the individual rooms inside the building were never locked. One father had his sons hang their wet jackets and gloves around a pot-bellied stove to dry after a snowball fight, but they put them too close. After they went to bed, the clothes began to smoulder. An older cousin went in later and found the room full of smoke. He opened the windows and saved them from smoke inhalation and possibly a serious fire.

One cousin remembers Hoy, Yip Kew Dang's fourth son, as being something of a pied piper because he was particularly inventive when it came to thinking up amusements. He'd also inherited his grandfather's knack for making money, once rigging up a scary haunted house and charging a one-penny entrance fee. Another time, Hoy and his cousin Wei, Yip Kew Ghim's oldest son, who was the same age as Hoy, set up a racetrack and used marbles for racehorses. Members of the audience placed bets on the marble "horses." Hoy sometimes borrowed eight-millimetre movies from a neighbour and charged his cousins five cents to attend the Saturday-night showings. He also started up a Wing Sang newsletter that he called "The Tiny Press." He made copies on a small printing press one of his brothers had given him for Christmas and charged a nickel for a one-month subscription. Contents included the results from the local sports teams and other items of general interest. After a while, the Christian Boy's Brigade allowed him to use their Gestetner machine to print off copies in exchange for the inclusion of a short, inspirational Bible message in his tabloid.

There was no money for lessons, but older cousins would teach whatever skills they had acquired. Cousin Yuey, Dang's second son, taught Bock, Ghim's second son, how to swim. Cousin Yen, Yip Kew Gin's older son, was an ace with a BB gun. Cousin Hoy could shoot while standing on one leg and using only one hand. Cousin Yen gave piano lessons and formed a musical group with his cousins Dennis and Stan Leong, Number Three Aunt Yip Gim Ying's oldest sons, who both played the saxophone, and Ben, Yip Kew Shuen's son, who played the drums. Sometimes the four of them played gigs at community functions or put on concerts. These always began with a rendering of "God Save the King," which was Britain's national anthem.

The cousins also participated in whatever the community had to offer. There was no community centre in Chinatown, but the local churches offered what they could to keep youngsters occupied and out of mischief. The Roman Catholic Church held boxing and badminton sessions. The Presbyterian Church organized basketball and Ping-Pong games. The Chinese United Church organized soccer games, classes on tumbling and, for the girls, a program called Canadian Girls in Training (CGIT). With no fixed religious affiliation, the cousins took advantage of all of these activities. The schoolroom in the Wing Sang building was also the meeting place for the 32nd Everest Boy Scout troop, and although outsiders were welcome, most of the scouts were Yips. The youngsters also went to friends' house parties. The female cousins' parents didn't worry about their daughters attending. They knew the Yip boys would look after them.

When it was time for students to leave for school, the house resounded with many pairs of feet thumping down the stairs, and sometimes the boys slid down the handrails. While they were too young to work, a group of the cousins spent school summer holidays at the saltery on Galiano Island. They slept in the bunkhouse and ate with the workers. They had a canoe, the ocean and room to play and explore. As they grew older, one of their uncles, who was a bookkeeper at a salmon cannery, made sure they were all hired for the summer holidays. Their regular pay was 8 to 10 cents per hour, but if they worked a 10-hour shift, they were paid 2 cents an hour overtime. If there was a big run of fish, they sometimes worked up to 20 hours in a 24-hour period. The youngsters could also find work digging potatoes or picking beans or strawberries for about 33 cents a day.

The youngsters didn't have all the fun. For the adults, there was frequently a birthday or baby banquet, a wedding or anniversary to celebrate, and if not, friends were invited for mah-jong or poker parties. While Yip Sang had disliked ostentation, he had always loved to have a good time. There were also funerals, and coming from a large family could make the timing of an engagement or wedding tricky, as these could not take place during the customary three-month period of mourning.

Traditions

One of the more traditional events held in the schoolroom was the introduction of a new wife with the tea ceremony. Maybelle, who married Yuey Wing Yip, Yip Kew Dang's second son, in 1952, remembers accompanying Lee Lei Yee, her mother-in-law, among the gathered family. As cups of tea were presented to each family member, in order of seniority, Maybelle bowed. The recipient of the tea then gave her an envelope containing a gift of money. The tea symbolized respect, and the bride's meeting with each of the groom's relatives symbolized that she was to become part of their family. The newlyweds also had their new married names written in Chinese calligraphy on a red silk banner that was hung in the schoolroom. They took the banner with them when they moved out of the family building and rented two furnished rooms for $10 a week. It wasn't easy to find somewhere to live, as many landlords wouldn't rent to Chinese Canadians. Everyone wanted to be paid cash too. The only places that accepted credit were department stores, which allowed customers 90 days to pay before they were charged interest.

A wife was expected to do whatever her mother-in-law said. Maybelle hadn't liked Chinese school, where she had learned little more than how to play Ping-Pong. Nevertheless, she was expected to send her own children, even though the Chinese school they attended believed in corporal punishment, and the teachers were mean. Families wanted children to learn their cultural heritage and be proud of being Chinese.

As part of this Chinese heritage, younger family members used birth order or the nature of their relationship to address older members. Yip Sang's grandchildren addressed uncles who were older than their father by the uncle's birth-order number and the word *bak* (meaning older uncle), as in Number Ten bak. Number Ten Uncle's wife would be Number Ten mo (with *mo* meaning older aunt). Uncles who were younger than their father would be addressed by their first name followed by *sook* (younger uncle). Number Twelve Uncle might be Yin sook, and Number Seventeen Uncle, Dock sook. Their wives would be the uncle's number followed by *som* (younger aunt) as in Number Twelve som and Number Seventeen som. Their father's sisters would simply be Number Two Aunt or Number Three Aunt, etc., depending on the aunts' birth order. Using the correct form of address was an important show of respect, or *xiao*.

Dances at the Yips' home were well attended and blended tradition with modern innovations. The great hall's wooden floor vibrated to the rhythms of the 78-rpm records played on the gramophone. There was always plenty of laughter and usually plenty to drink. However, the times most fondly remembered were Christmas and New Year's Eve. Yip Sang had believed in adopting western traditions, so New Year's Eve was celebrated on December 31.

Each family had its own Christmas tree, and at suppertime on Christmas Day the youngsters would make the rounds of each floor to wish their aunts and uncles a merry Christmas. On New Year's Eve, they sometimes attended parties thrown by friends, but always left around 11:30 PM so they could bring in the New Year at home. The family gathered there to let off strings of firecrackers, the men dressed in suits, the ladies in their colourful cheongsams. Then, in the schoolroom, they honoured their ancestors by bowing in front of the altar. The unmarried children in the families, even the 18- and 19-year-olds, visited their aunts and uncles, who handed out red paper envelopes containing lucky money or *licee*. The children, led by the older ones, would respond in unison, "Baba, Mama nin in ho, nin in fi lock jick do lo," which may be roughly translated to mean, "Papa, Mama every year bounty and happiness all the way to old age." After returning to their own rooms, they would then eat a meal that included long noodles, to denote long life, and treats such as oranges and homemade cookies. This particular tradition continued on until after the last grandmother, Wong Shee, died in 1957. Born in 1869, she was 88 years old and the longest lived of Yip Sang's wives. Dong Shee was born in 1865 and had died in 1941. Chin Shee was born in 1866 and died in 1934, just seven years after her husband.

Unlike Yip Sang, who wanted to adopt the traditions of his new country, many Chinese-Canadian families celebrated the Chinese New Year. This is also called the Spring Festival, as it marks the end of the winter season. It lasts for 15 days, ending with the Lantern Festival. The date of Chinese New Year's Day varies, falling between January 21 and February 20 on the Gregorian calendar, which was adopted by the Chinese in 1912. If Chinese-Canadian parents wanted their children to be excused from school on their New Year's Day, they had to write a letter for the teacher, however Yip Kew Dang wouldn't do this, so his children had to go to school.

Life in the Wing Sang Building

Families paid $5 a month to stay in the Wing Sang building. This went towards the water and electricity bills. Rent from the street-level stores and, later, space on the second floor, covered other expenses. Although the cousins had a lot of fun and received much encouragement and support from other family members, there were sometimes arguments, and they had to learn to share. As well as bedrooms, each floor of the building had two kitchens, two toilets and one bathtub. Most of the rooms were heated by pot-bellied stoves that burned wood or coal. Number Six Uncle, Yip Kew Gin, often sat inside the entrance to the building, where he could make sure incoming youngsters carried a load of wood or coal upstairs. When a fresh delivery of wood arrived, family members sometimes came close to fighting as they rushed down to pick out the best logs.

The taps delivered only cold running water, so bathwater had to be heated on a stove and carted to the bathtub in the unheated bathroom. The male Yips took their baths at the local bathhouse. Two telephones were eventually installed in the halls, one on the fourth floor and one on the sixth floor. If the call was for someone on the fifth floor, whoever answered had to yell up or down to get them. The phones made it possible for orders of meat and vegetables to be phoned in to suppliers and delivered to the home. Even though the Chinatown poultry stores had live chickens on the sidewalks so that customers could choose which one they wanted, the Yips had them delivered already plucked, dressed and ready to cook.

Changing Fortunes

Yip Sang's family likely fared better than most other Chinese-Canadian families during the 1930s and 1940s. The children thought nothing of wearing hand-me-down clothing, like their classmates. They always had something to eat, and children and adults alike had each other for support and camaraderie. Nevertheless, these decades brought significant changes to the way they lived.

If Yip Sang's sons had one complaint, it was that their lives had been too sheltered. Their father had given them almost everything they needed—love, shelter, food, discipline, jobs and education—but he'd kept tight control of his businesses and purse strings. When he died, he left his sons with no experience in handling or investing money. In a letter dated 1929, one son requested funds for his continuing education and expressed concern about family finances to one of his brothers. He asked for an unofficial statement and said that, as far as he knew, the family sources of income were fixed. While he recommended economy, he admitted that this would be unworkable for his generation. Aware that the grocery did not bring in much income and that investments needed to be expanded, he could also see that expenses were increasing as their family grew in size. He observed that the situation would be very bad if it remained the same for eight more years, which turned out to be true.

Even if Yip Sang's sons had inherited his facility for making money, it was almost impossible to expand investments during the Depression years, when unemployment was high and most people were lucky if they could feed their families from one week to the next. Grocery stores were common targets for theft. Property taxes were left unpaid, and family property was forfeited. As some of their businesses closed down, and the safety net of family money dissolved, family members tried to find work elsewhere. Maids were let go, and for the first time in their lives, family members had to fend for themselves. For women like Lee Lei Yee, Yip Kew Dang's wife, who had come from a wealthy family and never had to cook her own meals before, it was a difficult adjustment. Although she had four sons, only one lived in Vancouver, so this son's wife, Maybelle, had to do all Lee Lei Yee's errands and write all her letters.

When Yip Sang's grandchildren reached university age, it was still difficult for Chinese Canadians to work in many professions. Sun Wing Yip attended UBC and completed a bachelor of arts degree in 1939, a bachelor's degree in applied science in 1940 and a master's degree in 1941. His marks were good, but when companies sent headhunters to interview the 22 chemical engineering students during their final semester, Sun was the only student nobody interviewed. He wrote letters to several oil companies, but none of them offered him a job. He finally was offered a position at the Ashcroft Salt Company, which produced Epsom salts. There wasn't much future there, so he later found work on a tar-sands project and did some research. Eventually, someone suggested he apply for a job in a research laboratory for the Canadian Fishing Company. He worked there as manager of laboratories and technical research until he retired.

Wei Wing Yip took a degree in agriculture and another in accounting, becoming one of the first Chinese to practise as a chartered accountant. His younger brother Bock also became a chartered accountant. Bock graduated in 1960; nine years later, he was the youngest member ever elected to a fellowship in the Institute of Chartered Accountants of BC for conspicuous service to the profession. He was also the first Chinese Canadian to be elected into this exclusive group.

After serving in Canada's armed forces during the Second World War, brothers Peter and Fred Yip joined their older brother Roy in the grocery business. They began by taking over an uncle's store in Wells, and eventually their Royal Produce Company had 14 stores in different towns. Roy was working in one of the stores in Prince George in 1953 when the woodworkers' union went on strike. Taking a leaf out of his grandfather's book, he gave union members credit at the store until they went back to work three months later.

The Second World War

When Britain and France declared war on Germany following its invasion of Poland in September 1939, Canada's prime minister, William Lyon Mackenzie King, promised that there would be no conscription for overseas duty. All Canadians over the age of 16 had to take part in a national registration for war service, but compulsory military service was to be for the purpose of home defence only. As the war progressed, however, raids such as Dieppe and bitter struggles such as the February 1945 battle along the Hochwald Ridge resulted in heavy losses of Canadian troops. It became obvious that Mackenzie King would have to go back on his promise. The government held a national plebiscite, and all provinces except Quebec voted for conscription to military service overseas.

At first, recruits of Chinese background were signed up with other Canadians, but the government soon developed an official policy not to accept Chinese Canadians. Recruiting centres refused to sign them up, even as the need for men grew. A few tried to join up in the United States, but Canadian officials would not grant permits to allow this either. The issue was debated hotly in Vancouver's Chinatown. Some said that Chinese Canadians shouldn't be expected to fight for a country that treated them as second-class citizens and didn't allow them to vote in elections. Others said that if they fought for Canada, it would demonstrate their commitment to their country. How could they be refused the vote after putting their lives on the line, especially when a dozen or so veterans from the First World War had been given the right to vote?

If things hadn't gone so badly for the Allies, this debate would likely have been of no consequence, but in 1940, Hitler won victory after victory. With the fall of France and the demoralizing evacuation of Dunkirk, only the English Channel lay between Hitler's troops and Great Britain. Britain's prime minister, Sir Winston Churchill, wanted to co-ordinate all sabotage and subversive action against the enemy overseas. The Special Operations Executive (SOE) was formed to build and supply resistance movements in occupied territories. The men who volunteered for this resistance work would be their own masters and responsible for their own safety. It was dangerous work, and it was important that they be able to read and speak the local language.

The senior Canadian army commander in England, General A.G.L. McNaughton, was asked to loan three types of Canadian volunteers to the British War Office for service with the SOE. They wanted French Canadians for service in France, Canadians of eastern-European descent for operations in the Balkans, and Chinese Canadians for operations in Asia. The Canadian authorities had reservations about providing Chinese Canadians, foreseeing that they could hardly withhold the vote from citizens who had fought for Canada, but in 1941, with the situation growing more and more urgent, they agreed.

In Canada, the situation for Chinese Canadians was becoming awkward. They had to wear badges that identified them as Chinese because the Japanese were being moved out of Vancouver. In addition, people were asking why no Chinese Canadians were being called up to fight for their country. When British Columbia's Chinatown residents were asked to volunteer for duty, they were quick to respond. The young men had to be able to read and speak Chinese. They were told that a private was normally paid $30 per month, but they'd be paid $200 a month because their work would be so dangerous. If they were captured, the British and Canadian governments would deny any knowledge of them. They would likely be tortured, and the casualty rate was 80 percent.

Force 136

Thirteen young men signed up for Force 136, the cover name for the SOE in Southeast Asia. The volunteers were taken to a secret camp, Camp X, on Commando Bay near Penticton. They were taught the use of small arms, demolition, sabotage, silent killings, wireless communication and night operations. They were taught how to take an L pill, or suicide pill. These young men, who up until then had been barred from public swimming pools, were taught to swim so that they could attach explosives to ships' hulls. They were sent to Australia and India for further training in a tropical environment. Here they were taught not to walk or talk like soldiers, and they let their hair grow so they would blend in with the locals. They were originally intended to take part in Operation Oblivion in Japanese-occupied territories in south China, but General Douglas MacArthur claimed China as an American war zone. When their training was complete, they were parachuted into the Burmese jungle.

One 18-year-old soldier said that except for the training camps he'd barely been outside Chinatown. Now he was being parachuted into Japanese-occupied jungle to organize guerrilla fighters. If he hurt himself while landing, he would be left behind with his two L pills and no way out until the Allies arrived. Luckily, he landed unhurt, but to his horror, a man in a Japanese uniform rushed toward him. The young Chinese-Canadian soldier pulled out his revolver, but before he could shoot, the man in uniform shouted, "Friend, friend," in Chinese. He was a guerrilla fighter.

Unpleasant as the jungle was with its snakes and malaria-carrying mosquitoes, it also protected them. The guerrillas learned quickly, and they began to make hit-and-run attacks, firing at the Japanese for five minutes, then running away. Spying was harder. It required leaving the jungle to go into the town to try to glean useful information. The men felt more vulnerable away from the jungle, and on one occasion, a Canadian soldier was dismayed to realize he'd mistakenly worn his jungle boots into town. A Japanese soldier approached, and the Canadian, sweating and willing the Japanese not to notice his boots, couldn't look him in the eye. Luckily, the enemy solider passed him by without noticing anything unusual.

The initial volunteers performed so well that more Chinese Canadians were recruited for Force 136. One of the soldiers put on his uniform with the active service insignia on his sleeve and walked down Granville Street. For the first time in his life, he was treated with respect, and people moved aside so he could pass. Another group in uniform went to the local movie theatre and sat in the non-segregated section. No one asked them to move. The new recruits were in India waiting to be shipped out when the Americans dropped the atomic bomb on Hiroshima, so they were sent back to Canada instead.

The Canadian soldiers in Burma emerged from the jungle to accept the Japanese surrender and their weapons. They were also asked to help repatriate the emaciated prisoners of war. The initial group of 13 soldiers had all survived, and 4 were awarded the military medal for bravery.

Approximately 600 Chinese Canadians fought in the Second World War. A memorial plaque in Chinatown lists Vancouver's Chinese Canadians who served with Canadian Allied Forces. The list includes eight of Yip Sang's grandsons.

9

Transition

DURING THE WAR YEARS, Canadian workers produced raw materials, farm products and manufactured goods in unprecedented volumes. Such productivity put an end to the Depression, although some Chinese Canadians once again had difficulty finding work when returning soldiers took back their old jobs.

After returning home, Chinese-Canadian veterans lobbied Ottawa to recognize their status as legitimate Canadian citizens. Social attitudes were changing. Many Canadians were sympathetic toward the Chinese who had suffered under Japanese occupation. Chinese Canadians had raised a substantial sum of money for the war effort in China, and their young men had served their country. The veterans' campaign was successful; they were given the vote, thus paving the way for the rest of the Chinese community.

Chinese Canadians also lobbied to have the Chinese Immigration Act repealed, arguing that separating families was contrary to all principles of humanity and violated the proposed Universal Declaration of Human Rights in the United Nations Charter. The act was repealed in 1947, almost two years before the declaration was adopted in 1948. Families could finally be reunited, although limitations on the number of immigrants from China continued for years. It typically took two years for immigration paperwork to be completed, and only Chinese who were Canadian citizens could sponsor spouses and unmarried children; if they first had to become naturalized, it took even longer.

Alex Louie wrote a letter to the government in Ottawa. He said that he didn't expect the government to look after his aging mother. He simply wanted to point out that he and his two brothers had fought for the Allies, and it was time their mother was allowed home to spend her remaining years with them. She was finally permitted to return to Canada.

Along with the Chinese Immigration Act, the franchise restrictions were removed. By 1949, all eligible Chinese and East Indian–Canadians were allowed to vote in provincial and federal elections. Two years later, the Japanese were also allowed to vote. After the Second World War, Canada also began to develop a refugee policy for immigrants who could not prove they could support themselves. In 1962, the

Honourable Ellen Fairclough, minister of citizenship and immigration, introduced a new Immigration Act. It stated that unsponsored immigrants with the required education, skills or other desirable qualities should be allowed to enter Canada. There were still provisions that barred immigrants who did not have a job waiting or the means to support themselves while they found one, along with criminals, terrorists and people with diseases that could endanger the public health; however, those who were eligible would be admitted regardless of race, colour or national origin.

In 1967, a points system was established that judged potential immigrants on qualifications such as language and desirable skills. Nine years later, Canada's current Immigration Act was introduced. It encourages family reunification and accepts immigrants in four categories: close relatives of Canadian residents living in Canada; skilled workers and business people; those applying for humanitarian or compassionate reasons; and people escaping persecution, torture or other cruel or unusual punishment.

The People's Republic of China
While conditions for Chinese Canadians gradually improved in the post-war years, changes were taking place in China too. Although Dr. Sun Yat-sen didn't embrace communism, he collaborated with the emerging Communist Party to continue the fight for a republic. When the doctor died in 1925, Chiang Kai-shek took over leadership of the Nationalist Army

and by 1927 had decided to destroy the Communist Party. By 1930, civil war once more enveloped China and was complicated by an invasion by the land-hungry Japanese. Chiang Kai-shek concentrated on defeating the communists, but this didn't win him any support from the Chinese people, who hated the Japanese and wanted to defeat them. Eventually, the Americans took care of the Japanese, and after a long period of manoeuvring and fighting, Chiang Kai-shek was beaten and withdrew to Taiwan. On October 1, 1949, Mao Zedong proclaimed the People's Republic of China. Although Sun Yat-sen had not achieved his goal, he was posthumously declared the Founding Father of the Republic of China for his role in bringing an end to the Qing Dynasty.

Paper Sons
The republic did not resolve China's problems. Faced with unstable economic and political situations, many Chinese still wanted to leave their homeland. The old Canadian Immigration Act had been repealed, but the Chinese were still subject to the restrictions placed on all Asians and could only immigrate if they had immediate family members in Canada who were willing to sponsor them. As a result, some Chinese Canadians sold their children's birth certificates on the black market, whether those children were dead or still living. Many immigrants who moved to Canada at this time used fictitious names, incorrect ages and false marriages. These immigrants became known as "paper sons."

On June 9, 1960, Ellen Fairclough announced the Chinese Adjustment Statement Program. This granted amnesty for paper sons and daughters who confessed to entering the country illegally. About 12,000 immigrants came forward during the amnesty period, which ended in October 1973.

The Yips Leave Home

Wong Shee was the only one of Yip Sang's wives to live through the Second World War and experience Canada's coming of age. The world was changing, although change came slowly to the Wing Sang building. Younger members inherited the rooms staked out by their parents in their large home. Respect and obedience to one's elders meant respecting not only members of an older generation but also older members of one's own generation. Older aunts and uncles had authority over younger ones. Sometimes Number Four Uncle's visiting grandchildren would take Number Twelve Uncle's wife's pots and pans out of the cupboard and pretend they were drums, hitting them so hard they became dented. However, the wife, Bertha, never said anything. She waited until the grandchildren had gone home and then put her pots and pans away again.

Milk was delivered to the home, but Dana, Dang's oldest granddaughter, remembers being sent to buy bread and being admonished to make sure it was fresh. She and her brother Graeme also had fond memories of the Wo Fat Bakery, which rented one of the main-floor shops. The baker made the best-ever Buddha cookies, which were coloured with red food colouring. They had a soft gingerbread-like texture and sold three for five cents in an oily bag. Sometimes there were cookies in the shape of a little pig in a bamboo cage. Later, the bakery moved to Hastings Street. By that time, it was the only authentic Chinese bakery in Vancouver.

By the 1950s, family members had begun to move out of the Wing Sang building even though some people still wouldn't rent apartments or sell homes to Canadians of Chinese origin. Yuey and Maybelle, Dang's second son and his wife, bought a house in Mount Pleasant. When Dana and Graeme went back to visit Number Six Uncle, Yip Kew Gin, he was usually sitting in the store where his father had once sat and often gave them each a quarter. The school-room was one of the few places they were allowed to play.

The Wing Sang building had always been gloomy by modern standards, and stairways were not well lit. After electricity was installed in the building, the fuses had a tendency to blow, especially at Christmas time when each family had a Christmas tree. This was likely why only 15-watt light bulbs were used along the stairway, or perhaps the uncles, who always turned off the lights, wanted to keep the electricity bills down. The younger members of the family found the dark, creaky stairways scary, especially at the empty second floor, where the only sound was a clock ticking off the minutes. Great-granddaughter Sylvia kept up her courage by singing loudly as she climbed to the third floor.

Great-granddaughter Karin ran up the stairs as fast as she could when she visited her grandparents after regular school finished and before Chinese school began. It wasn't only the girls who were afraid either—all the children had heard stories of Number Four Uncle, Yip Kew Shuen, claiming he'd seen his father's ghost there, as well as that of the cook-handyman who had died in his bed on the second floor.

Equality at Last

In 1967, potential Chinese immigrants finally began to be processed under the same regulations as other immigrants to Canada, and in 1984, the Chinese-Canadian National Council launched a campaign for redress from the Canadian government for past head-tax payments. Ten years later, the government rejected this call for redress, but on June 22, 2006, Prime Minister Stephen Harper delivered an apology in the House of Commons. The first phrase of the apology was spoken in Cantonese. Mr. Harper announced that living Chinese head-tax payers or living spouses of deceased payers would be given a payment of $20,000 each. The government also set up a fund for community projects that acknowledge the impact of past wartime measures and immigration restrictions on ethnocultural communities. Some Chinese-Canadian families believe that the sons and daughters of head-tax payers should also be compensated, and they continue to fight for further redress.

The Wing Sang Company Building as it looked in 2010, 11 years after it was designated a heritage building. FRANCES HERN

Canada's Chinatowns Today

As Canadians of Chinese heritage found their place in mainstream society, Canada's Chinatowns went into decline. They were no longer the only sources of Chinese goods and services.

Vancouver's Chinatown had already undergone much

change since Yip Sang's days. By the mid-1920s, the Shanghai–Canton Alley complex was overcrowded, and health problems were developing. Although white business-men didn't want the Chinese moving onto their turf, the bustle of Chinatown life gradually shifted eastward toward Main and Pender Streets. By 1938, Canton Alley was owned by the city, although the Yip family still leased the lots. A warehouse was erected there in 1949, and the alley all but dis-appeared until 1998, when a social-services centre, the Chinese Benevolent Association Manor and the Vancouver Chinatown Merchants Association headquarters were built. Other build-ings and warehouses encroached on Shanghai Alley, and in 1995 it was extended westward to meet Taylor Street.

Part of Toronto's historic Chinatown was destroyed to make way for new buildings, including city hall. Calgary's Chinatown was forced to move twice but, anchored by its majestic cultural centre, is now thriving. In 1978, the mayor of Victoria asked whether his city's Chinatown should be preserved or demolished. Fortunately, residents realized the historical significance of Canada's oldest Chinese commu-nity, and it has been preserved. A new road resulted in part of Quebec City's Chinatown being demolished, and Vancouver's Chinatown might have met with the same fate but for a successful campaign to save it. In 1971, it was declared a his-torical area, and while its many neon signs became victims of a 1974 sign bylaw, it is now being revitalized.

Epilogue

FOLLOWING THEIR CHANGE in circumstances, the family reorganized the Wing Sang Company in 1950 and renamed it Yip Sang Ltd. Over the years that followed, family members moved out of the Wing Sang building to other parts of Vancouver and beyond. The empty space was rented out to restaurants and organizations. By the early 1970s, the old building no longer met city health and safety regulations, and renovations would have been expensive. When the one remaining aunt, Number Five Uncle's wife, Lee Lan Fan, moved out, it could have been the end of the 110-year-old building. Fortunately, people realized its historic importance, and in 1999 the City of Vancouver designated it a heritage building worth preserving for the role it had played in the city's past.

Epilogue

The building was sold in 2001. Bob Rennie, the new owner, was required to keep the red and yellow frontage intact. He also kept the stairway and schoolroom as they were. The schoolroom had been painted white and green because the Yip name means "green leaf." A divination to and from the ancestors remains painted on one of the schoolroom blackboards; it includes Chinese characters for the words celebration, happiness, longevity, plenty, prosperity and wealth. Rennie converted the rest of the front building into offices and hollowed out the upper five floors of the back building to make space for a private art gallery and museum. Because of its heritage-building designation, the exterior of the building had to be left intact, so Rennie put a complete new concrete liner inside, basically creating a new building inside the old one.

In April 1990, before the sale took place, the Yips cleared out items that had been stored inside the building for many years. The outer doors of a large walk-in safe had rusted shut, and a safecracker was employed to cut them open, along with a smaller safe that was found to be empty. Unfortunately, the contents of the larger safe were damp and mouldy due to a leaky ceiling, but four boxes of documents were salvaged.

Over 300 artifacts that help to tell the story of Vancouver's Chinatown were donated to the Museum of Vancouver. These included Yip Sang's ticket wicket. Photos were transferred to the City of Vancouver Archives, while documents found a home in the Chung Collection at UBC. Among these documents were letters dated from 1902 to 1918 that had been left for pickup at the Wing Sang building. Unable to trace the addressees, Yip family members had tied them in bundles for each year and kept them unopened. They were opened by the project's archivist in 1993. Written in old-style Chinese, their translation proved to be a challenge.

Some of the letters were enquiries about job opportunities and asked what life was like in Vancouver. Most were from families urging a husband or father to come home because his help was needed or because he was desperately missed, or from an elderly father wanting his son to return to take over his business. Some begged for money because a family member wanted to start up a business or couldn't make ends meet. Some were complaints to sons who hadn't sent money home in months, or they urged sons to work hard and avoid pitfalls, such as gambling, or to come home and marry. No one knows if the writers of these letters ever heard from their loved ones again.

In 2006, one of Yip Sang's Canadian great-grandsons visited China with his wife, son and daughter. They don't speak Chinese, but they undertook some research before they left Canada and were able to visit the Taishan No. 1 Middle School. It is now a high school attended by over 3,000 of the province's most promising students. The Canadian Yip family were also able to visit Sing Tong (Shentang), the village where Yip Sang was born. The name Shentang is a

The gate to Sing Tong (Shentang) village where Yip Sang was born. DOUG YIP

translation from the Mandarin name, but the Cantonese romanized translation is Sing Tong. This village, with around 200 inhabitants, is one of 23 that, along with a more modern area, make up Duhu County. Each of the villages has a gate to mark its boundary. The former Chinese Yip family memorial hall near the village entrance is now used as the seniors' recreation centre.

Yip Sang's oldest son, Number One Uncle, Yip Kew Yow, who was born in China, later returned to live in Sing Tong. Yip Kew Yow's son still lives there, and the son's grandson, Yip Sang's great-great-grandson, is a student at Taishan No. 1 High School. Both the great-great-grandson and his grandfather have since contacted the visiting Canadian Yip family.

Yip Sang made Canada his home, and unlike many of the Chinese who died in British Columbia before him, he asked that his remains be left to rest in Vancouver, instead of being shipped back to China. He is buried in Mountain View Cemetery, not far from his home on East Pender Street, and is surrounded by his second, third and fourth wives, several of his sons, a daughter-in-law and a couple of grandsons. Beyond the grass and trees rise the North Shore Mountains. While they didn't turn out to be made of gold after all, Yip Sang was still able to make his fortune through perseverance, hard work and an eye for opportunity. Other Canadians have succeeded by using such qualities, but few have started with so little or faced such challenging circumstances. Even though the money didn't last, he left behind a valuable legacy: the ideals of humanitarianism, honesty and self-improvement that he instilled in his heirs, and, of course, the part he played in British Columbia's history.

Significant Dates in Chinese-Canadian History

1850–64 Thousands of civilians are killed in China during the Taiping Rebellion.

1856–60 China loses the second Opium War and is forced to sign the Treaty of Nanking.

1858 The first Chinese gold miners arrive in the colony of British Columbia from San Francisco, after gold is discovered in the Fraser Valley.

1864 Yip Sang, aged 19, sails to San Francisco.

1866 The colony of British Columbia is joined with Vancouver Island to become a province, with Victoria as its capital.

1867 The British North America Act creates the Dominion of Canada on July 1.

1871 British Columbia is admitted to Canada as her sixth province.

1872 The British Columbia Qualification and Registration of Voters Act denies Chinese and First Nations peoples the right to vote.

1880 CPR contractor Andrew Onderdonk begins to hire Chinese labourers for railway work.

1881 Yip Sang leaves San Francisco for the Canadian goldfields.

1882 Yip Sang is employed by a CPR supply company in Vancouver. He supplies several thousand Chinese immigrants to help build the railway.

1885 The CPR is completed at Craigellachie, BC, on November 7.

1885 To discourage Chinese immigrants, the Chinese Immigration Act introduces a $50 head tax.

1885 Yip Sang returns to China and marries three wives. His first wife has two children.

1888 Yip Sang returns to Vancouver, leaving his wives and children in China. He sets up a merchant business called the Wing Sang Company.

1889 Yip Sang builds the Wing Sang Company building at 29 Dupont Street.

1891 Yip Sang becomes a naturalized British subject.

1900 The failed Boxer Rebellion in China results in an expanded Open Door policy.

1901 Yip Sang extends the Wing Sang building, and his wives and children join him in Vancouver.

1903 The head tax is raised to $500 per person.

1908 Yip Sang is one of the wealthiest merchants in Vancouver's Chinatown.

1911 China's last emperor is stripped of all power. A struggle for control of China ensues.

1910 Following the 1907 riots, a new immigration law is introduced. Increased restrictions include the "continuous journey" regulation.

1912 Yip Sang now has three wives and 23 children. He adds a six-storey building to the Wing Sang building. His businesses thrive, and he takes on philanthropic projects.

1914 The First World War breaks out. British Columbia refuses to allow Chinese Canadians to join the armed forces. Labourers from China are recruited into a Chinese Labour Corps.

1923 The Chinese Immigration Act is introduced on July 1. Chinese immigrants are banned from entering Canada, with only a few exceptions.

1927 Yip Sang dies at the age of 81.

1929 The New York Stock Exchange crashes in October. North America sinks into the Depression.

Significant Dates in Chinese-Canadian History

1930s Drought hits the prairies. These years become known as the Dirty Thirties.

1933 Twenty-seven percent of the Canadian population is unable to find work. The Yip family fortune is eaten away.

1939 The Second World War breaks out. Chinese-Canadians volunteer to join Force 136.

1939 Wartime productivity brings an end to the Depression.

1945 The Second World War ends. Chinese-Canadian veterans lobby for equality.

1947 The Chinese Immigration Act is repealed. Families are reunited and Chinese Canadians are allowed to vote.

1948 The last of Yip Sang's 81 grandchildren is born.

1949 Mao Zedong proclaims the People's Republic of China on October 1.

1960 Canada grants amnesty for "paper sons" on June 9.

1962 Canada's new immigration act admits qualifying immigrants regardless of race, colour or national origin.

1967 Potential Chinese immigrants are processed under the same regulations as all other immigrants.

1982 The Canadian Charter of Rights and Freedoms makes it illegal to discriminate based on race, national or ethnic origin, colour, religion, sex, age, or mental or physical ability.

1999 The Wing Sang building is designated a heritage building.

2001 The Yip family sell the Wing Sang building.

2006 On June 22, Prime Minister Stephen Harper makes an official apology to Chinese Canadians. Surviving head-tax payers or their spouses are to be compensated.

Chinese-Canadian Pioneers

1861 Won Alexander Cumyow, the first recorded Chinese-Canadian baby, is born.

1942–45 William (Bill) Gun Chong is known as agent 50 in China while he works for MI9, a British intelligence unit. He is awarded the Order of the British Empire in 1946 for his courage and bravery.

1943 William K.L. Lore becomes the first Chinese-Canadian naval officer.

1944 Cedric Mah follows brother Albert to become a "Flying Tiger" after they are refused entry into the RCAF. They fly supplies into China along the treacherous Burma Hump and are later awarded the Distinguished Flying Cross. Cedric later becomes a bush pilot.

1945 Dock K. Yip becomes the first Chinese-Canadian male lawyer called to the Canadian bar.

1947 Mary Laura Wong, teletype keyboard operator in the Canadian Women's Army Corps, is one of the first three Chinese-Canadian women to receive Canadian citizenship.

1955 Margaret Gee becomes the first Chinese-Canadian female lawyer called to the Canadian bar.

1955 Norman Lim "Normie" Kwong, the first Chinese-Canadian in the Canadian Football League, is named Canada's Athlete of the Year. He goes on to become a four-time Grey Cup winner and serve as Alberta's Lieutenant-Governor from 2005 to 2010.

1957 Douglas Jung is elected as the first Chinese-Canadian Member of Parliament in the House of Commons.

1959 George Ho Lem becomes the first Chinese Canadian in Calgary to win a municipal election and become alderman. His mother is the first recorded female Chinese resident of Calgary.

1969 Bock W. Yip becomes the first Chinese Canadian elected to a Fellowship in the Institute of Chartered Accountants.

1976 Jean B. Lumb becomes the first Chinese-Canadian woman and first restaurateur to receive the Order of Canada for her community work.

1995 Bing Wing Thom is named a Member of the Order of Canada for his award-winning architecture.

1998 Vivienne Poy becomes the first Chinese Canadian appointed to the Senate.

1999–2005 Adrienne Clarkson serves as the first Chinese-Canadian Governor General of Canada.

1999–2008 Alan Lowe serves as the first Chinese-Canadian mayor of Victoria.

2000 After winning many awards for his research in biochemistry, immunology and cancer genetics, Tak Wah Mak is named an Officer of the Order of Canada.

2005 Wayson Choy, writer and teacher, is named a Member of the Order of Canada.

2007 Jim Chu is named the first Chinese-Canadian chief constable of the Vancouver Police Department.

2008–2011 Patrick Chan becomes a four-time Canadian men's figure skating champion and 2011 world champion.

Bibliography

Anderson, Kay J. *Vancouver's Chinatown*. Montreal: McGill-Queen's University Press, 1991.

Berton, Pierre. *Klondike*. Toronto: Penguin Books Canada Ltd., 1990.

_____. *The Last Spike*. Toronto: McLelland and Stewart, 1974.

_____. *The National Dream*. Toronto: McLelland and Stewart, 1974.

Bumsted, J.M. *Canada's Diverse Peoples*. California: ABC-CLIO Inc., 2003.

Chow, Lily. *Sojourners in the North*. Prince George: Caitlin Press Inc., 1996.

Choy, Wayson. *The Jade Peony*. Vancouver: Douglas & McIntyre Ltd., 1995.

Conrad, Margaret, and Alvin Finkel. *History of the Canadian Peoples: Beginnings to 1867*. Toronto: Copp Clark Ltd., 1998.

Leung, Chik-Wai, ed. *Yip Sang*. Hong Kong: Cheong Tai Type-setting & Press Co., 1973.

Lunn, Janet, and Christopher Moore. *The Story of Canada*. Toronto: Lester Publishing Limited and Key Porter Books Limited, 1992.

Ng, Wing Chung. *The Chinese in Vancouver, 1945–80*. Vancouver: UBC Press, 1999.

Walker, Barrington, ed. *The History of Immigration and Racism in Canada*. Toronto: Canadian Scholars' Press Inc., 2008.

Yee, Paul. *Blood and Iron: Building the Railway*. Toronto: Scholastic Canada Ltd., 2010.

_____. *Saltwater City*. Vancouver: Douglas & McIntyre, 2006.

Index

ancestor altar, 77, 78–79, 111

Boxer Rebellion, 63–64, 72, 136
British North America Act, 18, 135
burial, secondary, 59, 60

Canadian Pacific Navigation Company, 56
Canadian Pacific Railway (CPR), 16, 19–27,
    29–32, 36, 40, 56, 83, 135
Canton. See Guangzhou
Canton Alley, 58, 66, 129
Chang Toy, 46, 82–84
Chiang Kai-shek, 99, 123, 124
Chinatown, Vancouver, 38, 40, 42, 46, 55,
    64–66, 67–68, 83, 90–91, 92, 104, 107, 120,
    128–29, 131
Chinese Adjustment Statement Program, 125
Chinese Benevolent Association, 59, 60, 61, 129
Chinese Board of Trade, 58
Chinese-Canadian National Council, 127
Chinese Empire Reform Association, 81–82
Chinese Freemasons Society, 61–62, 73
Chinese Immigration Act
    of 1885, 36, 135
    of 1923 (Chinese Exclusion Act), 94, 97,
    122, 136, 137
Chinese Labour Corps, 95, 136
Chinese Nationalist Party. See Guomindang
Chinese New Year, 111–12
Chin Shee, 34, 49, 53, 75–76, 111
Cixi, Empress, 63, 64, 73
Confucius, 35, 78
Craigellachie, 31, 135

Daoguang, Emperor, 43
Depression, 90, 91, 98, 100–3, 114, 121, 136, 137
Dong Shee, 34, 48, 49, 51, 52–53, 75

Fairclough, Ellen, 123, 125
False Creek, 32, 38, 40, 103

First World War, 35, 94–96, 117, 136
foot binding, 51–52
Force 136, 118–20

Galiano Island, 47, 87, 108
Gastown, 32
Gold Mountain (Gum Shan), 7, 27
gold rush
    California, 10–11, 13
    Fraser River, 12–14, 80, 135
Guangdong Province, 4, 7, 8, 17, 28, 33–34, 80,
    82, 91
Guangxu, Emperor, 63, 73
Guangzhou (Canton), 28, 43, 71, 92
Guomindang (Chinese Nationalist Party,
    Kuomintang), 72, 73–74

Harper, Stephen, 127, 137
head tax, 35, 36–37, 45, 46, 49, 62, 64, 86, 97, 127,
    135, 136, 137

Kang Youwei, 81–82
King, William Lyon Mackenzie, 68, 116
Kuomintang. See Guomindang

Lee Lei Yee, 109, 114
Lee Piu, 16
Lee Shee, 48, 50, 52, 53, 79
Leong, Dennis and Stan, 107
Lin Zexu, 43–44
Louie, Alex, 96, 122

Macdonald, John A., 18, 19, 20, 23, 30
Mackenzie, Alexander, 20
Mao Zedong, 124, 137
Mount St. Joseph Oriental Hospital, 71

Nanaimo Packing Company, 47

Onderdonk, Andrew, 22, 23, 135

141

opium, 41–45, 58, 61, 62, 68–69, 84
Opium and Narcotic Drug Act (1929), 68–69
Opium Wars, 27, 42–45, 63, 135
Oy Kuo Night School, 77

Pacific Scandal, 19–20
paper sons, 124–25, 137
People's Republic of China, 123–24, 137
polygamy, 48–49
Port Moody, 20, 22, 32
Punti, 33–34
Puyi, Emperor, 73, 74

Qianlong, Emperor, 49
Qing Dynasty, 27, 35, 61, 74, 124
Qualification and Registration of Voters Act
    (1872), 35

Rennie, Bob, 131

salt herring and salteries, 46–47, 83, 87, 88,
    91, 108
Sam Kee Company, 47, 66, 83–84
scurvy, 26
Second World War, 64, 82, 115, 116–20, 122,
    125, 137
Shanghai Alley, 58, 65, 66, 68, 73, 129
Sing Kew Theatre, 65, 66, 67–68, 73
Sing Tong (Shentang), 132, 133, 134
Sun Yat-sen, Dr., 62, 72–73, 123, 124

Taiping Rebellion, 27, 33, 135
Taishan No. 1 Middle School, 71, 132, 134
tea ceremony, 108–9
Treaty of Nanking, 44, 135

Universal Declaration of Human Rights
    (United Nations Charter), 122

Van Horne, Sir William Cornelius, 21, 30, 56

Wing Sang building, 38, 39, 40, 42, 48, 55,
    70, 75–76, 83, 100, 107, 112, 125–27, 128,
    130–32, 136, 137
Wing Sang Company, 37–38, 39, 40–41, 47,
    55–56, 69, 83, 128, 130, 136
Won Alexander Cumyow, 80–82, 138
Wong Shee, 34, 48, 50, 51, 53, 75–76, 111, 125

Yip
    Ben Wing, 107
    Bock Wing, 106, 115, 139
    Dana Gwynne, 125, 126
    Fred Wing, 115
    Gim Ling (Susan), 91, 92
    Graeme Gene, 125, 126
    Hoy Wing, 106–7
    Karin Paige, 127
    Kew Art, 91, 92
    Kew Dang, 87, 88–89, 112
    Kew Dock, 91, 92–94, 138
    Kew Ghim, 92
    Kew Gin, 112, 126
    Kew Him, 89
    Kew Lap, 87
    Kew Ming, 89
    Kew Mow, 91, 93
    Kew Park, 88
    Kew Quene, 89, 90, 91
    Kew Sheck, 88, 89
    Kew Shuen, 127
    Kew Suey, 100
    Kew Yow, 100, 134
    Kew Yacht, 89
    Maybelle, 108–9, 114, 126
    Peter Wing, 115
    Roy Wing, 115
    Sun Wing, 77, 100, 114–15
    Sylvia, 126
    Victoria (Chow), 93
    Victoria (Lore), 91
    Wei Wing, 115
    Yen Wing, 106, 107
    Yuey Wing, 106, 108, 126
Yip Sang
    businesses, 37–41, 46–47, 48, 55–56, 66,
        69–70, 81
    and his children, 77, 84–85, 87–88
    death and funeral, 98–100
    and gold rushes, 10–11, 14, 15
    marriages, 34
    philanthropy, 60, 65, 69, 70 71, 76
    and railway, 16–17, 22, 29
    travels to China, 33–34, 35
    travels to North America, 7–8
Yongzheng, Emperor, 42
Yuan Shikai, 74

Acknowledgements

I couldn't have written this book without a great deal of help from Karin, Maybelle and Yuey Yip, but other family members have also helped me find answers to many questions. These include Dana and Wayne, Graeme, Doug, Sun, Aunt Molly, Wei, Mel and Shirley, Bock, Rosalee, Linda, Bing and Sylvia.

Thanks also go to Carol Haber at the City of Vancouver Archives, Sarah Romkey and Jaimie Miller who work with UBC's Wallace B. and Madeline H. Chung Collection, Carrie Schmidt and Bob Cuthbert at the Vancouver Maritime Museum Archives, Susan Kooyman and Adria Lund at the Glenbow Museum Archives, the helpful librarians at the main branch of the Vancouver Public Library, editors Vivian Sinclair and Lesley Reynolds, who helped bring this book to life, and Bill Pitcher at Golden Photography for providing the author's photograph. Last, but definitely not least, thanks to Keith, who delivered pre-dinner glasses of wine upstairs to my writing desk and cooked me many dinners while I pieced together the Yip family history.

Few of Yip Sang's surviving descendants actually met their patriarch, so their knowledge of him has been passed down from other family members; sources are sometimes unclear, conflicting or incomplete. It seems certain that Yip Sang left a brother behind in China, but I have been unable to discover what happened to him. I would be pleased to hear from anyone who has additional information. I can be contacted care of heritage@heritagehouse.ca.

Bill Pitcher, www.williampitcher.ca

About the Author

Frances Hern writes poetry, fiction and non-fiction. History was not one of her favourite subjects at school, so it is ironic that much of what she now writes is inspired by historical events that interest and intrigue her.

Yip Sang is her third Amazing Stories title. She also wrote *Arctic Explorers*, which details the 400-year search to find the elusive Northwest Passage, and *Norman Bethune*, a biography of the Canadian doctor who thought that everyone should be entitled to receive medical care, regardless of their station in life. For more information, check out her website: www.franceshern.ca.